MUSTANG BON FOUNDATION

These advanced practices should only be practiced after getting the appropriate transmission, and done only by practitioners with appropriate qualifications, permissions, and pith instructions. Without such qualifications, permissions, and instructions these practices can be dangerous, so do not put yourself at risk.

Heart Drops of Kuntuzangpo

ISBN: 978-1-956950-10-6
Library of Congress Control Number: 2019941163

Copyright © 2022 Mustang Bon Foundation
All rights reserved. No part of this book may be reproduced without prior written permission from the publisher.

Published by Mustang Bon Publishing

Second Edition

Front cover: Shardza practicing rainbow body (source unknown)

MustangBonFoundation.org

Printed and Bound in the United States of America

Layout and design by Brad Reynolds integralartandstudies.com

Heart Drops
of Kuntuzangpo

Shar rdza bKra' shis rGyal mtshan
(Shardza Tashi Gyaltsen)
1859 – 1934

Herein is the Explanatory Practical Guide on the Clear-Light of the Stages of the Bon Dzogchen Path Known as

"Heart Drops of Kuntuzangpo"

Written by
Shardza Tashi Gyaltsen
(1859 – 1934)

Translated under the guidance of
His Holiness the thirty-third
Menri Trizin

by Geshe Sonam Gurung
and Daniel P. Brown, Ph.D.

For Pointing Out the Great Way Foundation

*May the translation of these precious lineage teachings
cause their benefits to flourish everywhere
and serve the welfare of all beings.*

Geshe Sonam Gurung grew up in an indigenous Bon Tibetan region of Nepal, in the Pangling Village area of Central Mustang. When he was nine years old he was sent by the local Bon lama to become a monk at Menri Monastery, the seat of the indigenous Bon religion, now located in the Dolanji area of India. He spent fourteen years obtaining his Geshe degree (the equivalent of a doctoral degree in Bon spiritual studies) under the guidance of His Holiness Menri Trizin, the spiritual leader and lineage holder of the Bon and the 33rd Head Abbott of Menri Monastery. After obtaining his Geshe degree he served as treasurer, guest master, and personal assistant to His Holiness Menri Trizin at Menri Monastery. Recently, Geshe Sonam returned to the Jomsom area of Central Mustang to reestablish and spread the indigenous Bon teachings in his country of origin. Two documentaries have been made about Geshe Sonam's life and work: *Bon: From Mustang to Menri*, and a follow-up film about his return home, *Returning the Blessings*.

Daniel P. Brown, Ph.D. is an Associate Clinical Professor in Psychology, Dept. of Psychiatry, at Harvard Medical School at Beth Israel Deaconess Medical Center. He has been on the HMS faculty for 37 years, where he teaches a variety of clinical assessment and treatment courses and also a course on performance excellence for physicians, CEOs, and judges. In graduate school at the University of Chicago he studied Sanskrit, and at the University of Wisconsin he studied Tibetan, Buddhist Sanskrit, and Pali. In the 1980s he wrote *Transformations of Consciousness* with Ken Wilber and Jack Engler. He is also the author of *Pointing Out the Great Way: The Stages of Meditation in the Mahamudra Tradition*, and two books on public dialogues with H.H. the Dalai Lama. More recently, under the guidance of H.H. Menri Trizin, he and Geshe Sonam translated Bru rGyal ba g.Yung drung's *The Pith Instructions for the Stages of the Practice Sessions of Bon rDzogs Chen [Great Completion] Meditation*, and a collection of eleven advanced yogic texts, Shar rdza bKra' shis rGyal mtshan's *sKu gsum rang shar [Self-Arising Three-fold Embodiment of Enlightenment]*.

Table of Contents

Acknowledgments xiii

INTRODUCTION 1
Preliminary Meditation Practice in the *Heart Drops* 2
The Actual Foundational Practices 5
Thoroughly Cutting Through Practice 5
By-Passing 10
Great and Standard Consciousness-Transference 16

1.0 **Preliminaries** 24
1.1 **Distinguishing Between Saṁsāra and Nirvāṇa** 24
1.1.1 **External Practices** 25
1.1.2 **Internal Practices** 26
1.2 **Reversing Attachment to the Body and Mind as Objects by Training the Three Gateways—Body, Speech, and Mind** 26
1.2.1 **Body Practice** 26
1.2.2 **Speech Practice** 27
1.2.2.1 **Sealing Speech** 27
1.2.2.1.1 **External** 28
1.2.2.1.2 **Internal** 28
1.2.2.1.3 **The Purpose of Sealing** 28
1.2.2.2 **Skillful Practice** 29
1.2.2.2.1 **External** 29
1.2.2.2.2 **Internal** 29
1.2.2.2.3 **The Purpose of Skillful Practice** 30
1.2.2.3 **Practicing Pliancy** 30
1.2.2.3.1 **External** 30
1.2.2.3.2 **Internal** 30
1.2.2.3.3 **Purpose** 31
1.2.2.4 **Engaging as Path** 31
1.2.2.4.1 **Etymology** 31

1.2.2.4.2 **The Skillful Means of Practicing the Meditation** 31
1.2.2.4.3 **The Purpose** 32
1.2.3 **Mind Practice** 32
1.2.3.1 **The Nine Skillful Means to Determine Mind as Awakened Mind-Itself** 32
1.2.3.1.1 **Examine and Search Your Own Mind as Empty** 33
1.2.3.1.2 **Examine and Search Into Appearances** 33
1.2.3.1.3 **Examine and Search Appearances as Without Inherent Nature** 33
1.2.3.1.4 **Examine and Search Appearance/Emptiness as Transcending All Limits** 34
1.2.3.1.5 **Examine and Search as Existing** 34
1.2.3.1.6 **Examine and Search as Non-Existing** 34
1.2.3.1.7 **Examine and Search as Not Existing as Either** 35
1.2.3.1.8 **Examining and Searching Into the Basis** 35
1.2.3.1.9 **Search the Basis as Never Lost and as Without [Substantiality]** 35
1.2.3.2 **The Basis of Mind in Coming, Staying, and Going** 36
1.2.3.2.1 **Coming** 36
1.2.3.2.2 **Staying** 37
1.2.3.2.3 **Going** 38
2.0 **Actual Foundational Practices** 39
2.1 **Methods for Entering the Gateway of the Path** 39
2.1.1 **The Way to Establish a Connection to the Teaching on the Practical Guide of the Actual Path** 39
2.1.2 **Detailed Explanation of the Actual Practice** 41
2.1.2.1 **Different Capacities** 41
2.1.2.1.1 **Lesser Capacity** 41
2.1.2.1.2 **Sharpest Capacity** 43
2.2 **Actual Practice; Thoroughly Cutting Through** 43
2.2.1 **The Actual Pointing Out For Liberation** 43
2.2.1.1 **Commenting on the Essential Point** 44
2.2.1.1.1 **Pointing Out the Root, Primordial Awakened Awareness** 44
2.2.1.1.1.1 **All-Encompassing Awareness** 44

2.2.1.1.1.2 Reflection on Awareness 44
2.2.1.1.1.3 Primordial Awakened Awareness 44
2.2.1.1.2 Pointing Out the Four—View, Meditation, Conduct,
　　　　Fruition 46
2.2.1.1.2.1 View 46
2.2.1.1.2.2 Meditation 48
2.2.1.1.2.3 Conduct 50
2.2.1.1.2.4 Fruition 51
2.2.1.2 Stopping and Tying Up 52
2.2.1.3 Binding 54
2.2.2 The Great Non-Action for Crossing Over 54
2.2.2.1 Explaining the General Meaning of Removing
　　　Faults 54
2.2.2.2 Explaining the Nature of Not Doing in Particular 55
2.2.2.2.1 The Four Aims 55
2.2.2.2.2 The Three Capacities of Confidence 55
2.2.2.2.3 The Five Phenomena for Crossing-Over via Not
　　　　Doing 56
2.2.2.2.3.1 No Buddhahood by the Phenomena of Doing 56
2.2.2.2.3.2 Without Relying on any Remedy 57
2.2.2.2.3.3 Whatever Arises is the Play of Primordial
　　　　　Wisdom 57
2.2.2.2.3.4 All Phenomena Arise From the Expanse of
　　　　　Dharmadhātu 57
2.2.2.2.3.5 Liberation From Extremes 58
2.2.2.3 Explaining the Confidence of Meditative Practice 58
2.3 Attaining the Truth—By-Passing 59
2.3.1 Why By-Passing is the Higher Way 60
2.3.1.1 Purifying Dualistic Grasping 60
2.3.1.2 The Distinction of the Self-Appearance of the
　　　Aggregates of the Physical Body 60
2.3.1.3 The Distinction of Purifying Consciousness 61
2.3.1.4 Serving the Purpose of Others by Directly Seeing
　　　the Clear-Light [From the Viewpoint that] Nothing
　　　Inherently Exists 61

2.3.1.5 **The Distinction of Not Searching for the Fruition** 62
2.3.1.6 **The Distinction of Directly Seeing the Self-Visions** 62
2.3.1.7 **The Distinction of the Levels [of Development]** 62
2.3.2 **Explaining the Actual Teaching for the Secret Path; The Essential Point of the Pith Instructions to Establish Certainty** 63
2.3.2.1 **Four Great Kings** 64
2.3.2.1.1 **The Essential Points of Body, Speech, and Mind** 65
2.3.2.1.1.1 **Body** 65
2.3.2.1.1.2 **Speech** 67
2.3.2.1.1.3 **Mind** 67
2.3.2.1.2 **The Essential Point of the [Eye] Gateways** 67
2.3.2.1.3 **The Essential Point of the Object [of Vision]** 68
2.3.2.1.4 **The Essential Point of Slowing Down the Winds and Awakened Awareness** 68
2.3.2.2 **Four Winds of Emanation—the Four Special Channels** 68
2.3.2.3 **Four Fires of Balancing the Temperature [The Four Lamps]** 70
2.3.2.4 **The Golden Earth and Eight Clear Mirrors** 71
2.3.2.5 **Four Great Rivers [Four Levels of Visions]** 72
2.3.2.6 **All the Stars and Planets** 75
2.3.2.7 **Five Radiant Lamps Generated from the Crown** 77
2.3.2.8 **Three Secret Seed-Syllables are Set in Mind** 78
2.3.2.8.1 **The Two Attainments** 80
2.3.2.8.1.1 **Free of Re-Birth** 80
2.3.2.8.1.2 **Great Consciousness-Transference** 80
2.3.2.9 **Final Support—Four Seasons and Four Queens** 82
2.3.2.9.1 **The Three Immovable Bases** 82
2.3.2.9.2 **The Three Stabilities** 82
2.3.2.9.2.1 **Signs Arising in the Three Gateways** 83
2.3.2.9.2.1.1 **Signs Directly Manifest in the *Dharmadhātu*** 83
2.3.2.9.2.1.1.1 **The Three Gates** 83
2.3.2.9.2.1.1.1.1 **Body** 83
2.3.2.9.2.1.1.1.2 **Speech** 83

2.3.2.9.2.1.1.1.3 **Mind** 83
2.3.2.9.2.1.2 **At the Time Previous Meditative Experiences Increase** 84
2.3.2.9.2.1.3 **At the Time Awakened Awareness Reaches Full Measure** 84
2.3.2.9.2.1.4 **At the Time of Dharmadhātu Exhaustion** 85
2.3.2.9.2.2 **Assessment of Dreams** 85
2.3.2.9.2.3 **The Three Attainments** 86
2.3.2.9.2.4 **The Four Confidences** 86
2.3.2.9.2.5 **The Four Servants Acting to Serve Him** 87
2.4 **Consciousness-Transference and After-Death Bardo Practices** 87
2.4.1 *Bardo* **of [Normal] Life** 87
2.4.2 *Bardo* **of the Time of Dying** 88
2.4.3 *Bardo* **of** *Dharmadhātu* 91
2.4.3.1 **Eight Visions** 93
2.4.3.2 **Three Teachings** 95
2.4.3.3 **Six Secondary Conditions that Remind You** 95
2.4.3.4 **Consciousness-Transference** 97

Bibliography 103

Acknowledgments

Our deepest gratitude to His Holiness the 33rd Menri Trizin. Without his support this work would never have been translated. Also, our deepest thanks to Kathleen McCarthy who did the initial copy editing on this manuscript, and to Susan Pottish who did the final stage of copy editing on this manuscript. Our deepest gratitude goes to Dustin DiPerna of Bright Alliance Publishers for the personal touch he gave to the publication of this precious set of teachings, and Brad Reynolds, the type-setter, for his masterful layout and sensitive handling of these complex scriptures Thanks also to Roger and Brenda Gibson, whose generous donation paid for the translation, and to the Pointing Out the Great Way Foundation for sponsoring these translation projects.

Introduction

Shar rdza bKra' shis rGyal mtshan is one of the greatest Bon scholars and meditation practitioners in the past thousand years. Among his collected works[1] he wrote a trilogy of important texts on Great Completion meditation. This massive opus on Great Completion is his *dByings rig mdzod* [*Treasury of the Expanse and Awakened Awareness*]—a thorough and comprehensive presentation on Bon Great Completion in twenty-one chapters. His other main work is his *sKu gsum rang shar* [*Self-Arising Three-fold Embodiment of Enlightenment*]—a description of advanced cave and hermitage yogi practices filling over eleven books.[2] The third, and smallest of his trilogy, is his *Kun tu bzang po'i snying tig* [*Heart Drops of Kun tu bZang po*]. The *Heart Drops* represents Shar rdza Rinpoche's most condensed version of the essential Bon Great Completion meditation practices. Our intention is to make all three of Shar rdza Rinpoche's works available to the West.

The *Heart Drops* was previously translated into English by Lopon Tenzin Namdak as the *Heart Drops of Dharmakaya: Dzogchen Practice of the Bon Tradition*.[3] However, that edition is not a line-by-line translation of the *Heart Drops*, but rather is a series of valuable lectures and oral teachings on the *Heart Drops*. It is not at all our intention to produce another translation that competes with this readily available and important work.

---

1. *Shar rdza' bKa' 'bum* [*The Collected Works of Shar rDza*]. Chamdo, 16 volumes. Block print version, (ca. 1990).

2. sKu gsum rang shar [*Self-Arising Three-fold Embodiment of Enlightenment*] in Shar rdza' bKa' 'bum [*The Collected Works of Shar rdza*]. Chamdo, 16 volumes. Block print version (ca. 1990). Found in volume *KHA*, pp. 1-402.

3. Shardza Tashi Gyaltsen, *Heart Drops of Dharmakaya: Dzogchen Practice of the Bon Tradition*, Ithaca, NY: Snow Lion, 1993.

However, that work, as an oral teaching, omits certain sections of the teachings, covers other sections too briefly, and systematically omits the other works Shar rdza Rinpoche cites to back up his main points. Therefore, we have decided to make a full, line-by-line translation of the *Heart Drops* available to qualified students. We strongly recommend that this line-by-line translation be used as a complement to, not a substitute for, the precious oral teachings by Lopon Tenzin Namdak in his version of the *Heart Drops*.

The *Heart Drops* is divided into four sections:

(1) Preliminary meditations,

(2) Thoroughly cutting through Great Completion meditation,

(3) By-passing Great Completion meditation, and

(4) Consciousness-transference.

As his most condensed text on Great Completion, the *Heart Drops* represents Shar rdza Rinpoche's distillation of his most important essential points about Great Completion, especially featuring the heart-essence of by-passing practice.

Preliminary Meditation Practice in the *Heart Drops*

The section on preliminary practices in the *Heart Drops* is anything but preliminary. These practices are designed to dismantle the substantiality of the external world, the physical body, and the mind, and to refine the fundamental experience and realization of emptiness at all times and in all situations, as applicable to all phenomena. Bon Great Completion divides the teachings into the mind-series, space-series, and pith instruction-series teachings. The preliminary section of the *Heart Drops* represents a distillation of the best of the mind-series teachings. Shar rdza Rinpoche divides these preliminary teachings into two areas:

(1) Distinguishing between *saṁsāra* and *nirvāṇa*, and

(2) Reversing attachment to the body and mind as objects by training the three gateways—body, speech, and mind.

The first teaching is based on the fact that the primordial *Buddha*, Kun tu bZang po, has "enlightened intention" (*dgongs*). In fact, as part of inherent *Buddha*-nature, all sentient beings also have enlightened intention, but it is usually clouded over by the seeming substantial structures of the ordinary mind. As a meditation, the practitioner imagines him- or herself as inseparable from the enlightened intention of Kun tu bZang po while imitating the unique behaviors and sufferings of each of the six classes of beings in *saṁsāra*—the hell realm beings, the hungry ghosts, the animals, the gods, the demi-gods, and the humans. Then, the practitioner imagines each of these six classes of beings receiving the Bon Great Completion teachings to subdue their mind-streams and guide them along the Great Completion path out of *saṁsāra* to be reestablished in awakened *dharmakāya* space. The essential point of the practice, however, is the refinement of the realization of emptiness. Emptiness meditation, as a practice, entails searching with awareness, not conceptual thought, to find the substantiality or inherent self-existence of some structure of mind, and searching thoroughly until experiencing the experiential shift of unfindability. The type of emptiness practice in the *Heart Drops* constitutes an "intense means" (*btsan thabs*) to reverse attachment to *saṁsāra* through the determination of the emptiness of all phenomena:

> The reason is that your instantaneous [ordinary] mind is the root of all *saṁsāra* and *nirvāṇa*. Therefore, by imitating the conduct of all the beings in the six classes of beings by these intense means and acting accordingly, find the agent [who is doing this conduct]. Through that, you will know that it depends on the mind, and that the agent is categorized as within the mind. Through knowing that, the ways [each of] the six classes of beings appear at this time are understood merely as the manifestations of the mind. Through knowing that, you will come to know the essence of the mind as being emptiness, and stop the cause of *saṁsāra*. Through stopping that, you will come to know the fruition of having stopped *saṁsāra* thereafter, [namely] not engaging in *saṁsāra* (83-84).

The second teaching is designed to "reverse attachment" (84) to *saṁsāra* using the three ordinary gateways of practice—body, speech, and mind. The body practice entails taking the *vajra* posture, which is designed to purify obscurations, protect the practitioner from demonic influences, and "directly stop attachment to the physical body" (85).

Speech-related practice entails four steps. First, "sealing" speech (*rgyas gdap pa*) entails imagining all externally appearing phenomena and the internal substance of the physical body as if composed entirely of seed-syllables, *HUNG*s, and thereby to be insubstantial. The purpose of the visualization is to realize the emptiness of all seemingly external appearing objects and the physical body so as to "liberate" the practitioner from attachment either to the external world or the physical body (87).

Second, "skillful practice" (*rtsal sbyong pa*) entails a more intense visualization using the seed-syllable *HUNG*. In this practice immeasurable *HUNG*s are imagined as "lightning bolts" (87) shot from the heart with "full force" (87) destroying the residual substantiality of all appearing external objects and the residual aggregates of the physical body. The sign of progress is the "full measure of mastery," wherein the residual substantiality of the world and body is experienced as disappearing.

Third, "pliancy" (*mnyen btsal pa*) is designed to develop stability of the realization to attain "the completely purified positive qualities" (89).

Fourth, "engaging as path" (*lam du gzhag*) is to extend the realization of emptiness to the pure *Buddha*-fields and open up the direct perception of these sacred realms of the *sambhogakāya* as always right here, seen instead of the ordinary deluded external world. As a culmination of these four sequential meditation practices, the practitioner directly establishes an experiential link with the *sambhogakāya* and begins to perceive not an ordinary world "out there" but the sacred world of the *mandala* as always right here.

Mind-related practices are two practices:

(1) The nine practices of emptiness to set up the determination of the mind's awakened awareness, and

(2) Cutting off the root of coming, staying, and passing of mental events.

With respect to the nine practices of emptiness, they include: searching the mind as empty until "it becomes totally empty like space" (91);

searching appearances as empty until they "unobstructedly" occur as emptiness/liveliness (92); searching into the nature of appearances as not having any substantial characteristics; dismantling any residual substantiality of appearances and the physical body until everything is realized as illusion-like (93); searching into what seems to remain as "existing," as "not existing," and as "neither existing nor not-existing" to develop a level of realization beyond the extremes of existing/not existing (93); searching to find any substantial basis to residual conceptual thought; and finally, searching into the awakened mind-itself as "without inherent nature" (95). The cumulative effect of this series of emptiness meditations sets up the direct realization of awakened-mind-itself. As Shar rdza Rinpoche says, the purpose of these emptiness meditations is "to come to the realization of awakened mind-itself" as "transparent," i.e., as obviously always right here (96).

The next practice, "the basis of the mind in coming, staying, and going" (96), is designed to extend the immediacy of the realization of emptiness to events as they begin to arise each moment, moment-by-moment. In this manner the experience of emptiness extends beyond ordinary coming and going in time to the direct experience of the limitlessness of awakened awareness. As Shar rdza Rinpoche says, "At this point in time on the path, the view becomes limitless" (97) so as to "directly become inseparable from non-duality and the *dharmakāya*" (100).

THE ACTUAL FOUNDATIONAL PRACTICES

In the *Heart Drops* there are three kinds of actual foundational practices—thoroughly cutting through practice, by-passing practice, and consciousness-transference practice.

THOROUGHLY CUTTING THROUGH PRACTICE

As the name, thoroughly cutting through practice, implies, the aim of such practice is to cut through the residual obscurations of the ordinary mind so as to directly realize the timeless, limitless, non-dual, and non-localized, lucid expanse of awakened awareness/compassion that is always right here, like the sun that always shines but is not perceived when it is covered by clouds. Emptiness *is* the path in the sense that the application of emptiness entails going beyond the clouds that obscure the realization of awakened awareness that is always right here. Thoroughly cutting through practice is described as "the gateway of entering the path" (100) in the sense that these precious pith instructions give the practitioner the necessary view and meditation instructions for opening the door to the direct experience of the awakened mind. Shar rdza Rinpoche makes it clear that receiving these precious pith instructions in Bon Great Completion depends on those practitioners of fortunate karmic connection and best capacity, who have transformed their mindstream, typically through completion of 100,000 preliminary practices, and who have received the gift-waves of influence or initiation from a qualified lama. He also begins with a note of caution, namely that in this current time there are many seemingly Great Completion practices that teach mistaken views and meditation practices. According to Shar rdza Rinpoche, the best thoroughly cutting through Great Completion practices are such that mistakes are cut off as soon as they arise. He says:

> In the *Ye khri mtha' sel* [*Removing the Extremes to the Primordial Throne*] it says, "The epitome of the Great Completion vehicle is [to realize] there is nothing to abandon, nor anything great to strive after. Don't strive for basis, path, and fruition [enlightenment]. You are liberated from grasping the [views of the] external and internal vehicles. It goes beyond abandoning or attaining some object of fruition. It is the basis of operation for those of best capacity" (101).

Furthermore, Shar rdza Rinpoche cautions that in current times, even those practitioners who are given unmistaken pith instructions are at risk of striving after a specific outcome or becoming attached to some idea about the final fruition. According to Shar rdza Rinpoche, the best instructions are to "go…beyond abandoning or attaining some object of fruition" (101). Shar rdza Rinpoche adds that this specific set of pith instructions offers gradual "practical guidance" so that the direct realization of awakened awareness occurs by-itself, to-itself (103). However, such instructions entailing "intense means" are not readily understandable for all practitioners, but are more likely to be especially effective for practitioners of "sharpest capacity" (103) for whom, through "total immersion" in their practice, the instructions are experienced like "an instant of lightning coming down," and for whom "the fruition will directly manifest itself in this very lifetime" (103).

The actual pith instructions are divided into two parts:

(1) The actual pointing out instructions, and

(2) Crossing-over with the great non-action.

The first pith instruction entails an introduction to the real nature of awakened awareness so as to increase the likelihood that the practitioner will directly realize the awakened mind as always right here. Shar rdza Rinpoche says, "This is the awakened awareness—whether you know it or not, or whether you meditate upon it or not" (107). The direct introduction to the awakened mind is given directly from the teacher to the student from heart-to-heart. Shar rdza Rinpoche says:

> The lama says [to the student], "Ah, fortunate child of the lineage! Look nakedly to see in yourself if there is any agent of your reflecting or of your being aware. Is there a duality between an agent of looking and an object looked at? Through turning inward and reversing the [dualistic] mind as non-dual, they occur by their own nature openly like space.
>
> In that, do not do anything to change even a hair of this, because the real nature of this is inexpressible; inseparable pairs of the clarity/emptiness and mind/appearance can never be impeded by any name whatsoever. You cannot know this by determining it by example, by expression, or by conceptually analyzing it. What is transparent cannot be abandoned. It is free of skillful means, without basis, rootless. It is all-pervasive emptiness. Its clarity is unobstructed. It is more and more awake. Its primordial liberation becomes more and more transparent. Its self-occurring brightness becomes clearer and clearer. Its bliss without an antidote becomes more and more vibrant. As primordially arisen, it is bare and more and more naked. Awakened awareness never knows distraction. Its clear-light is

without seeing. Its natural disposition is uninterrupted. Its nature can't be expressed in words. Its primordial wisdom can never be abandoned. Its lucid appearance is selfless. The sparkling immediacy of the mind is non-conceptual. Its primordial wisdom does not separate subject and object. This wakeful empty space and openness of mind without essence is the secret path of Great Completion (108-109).

According to Shar rdza Rinpoche, the lama introduces the "best view much like a roaring lion" (111).

The next set of pith instructions pertains to the view, meditation, conduct, and fruition. The purpose of introducing this specific set of instructions is to eradicate the residual effects of the ordinary mind on view, meditation, conduct, and fruition. For example, with respect to view, the aim is to realize the emptiness of the residuals of a self or mind setting up or holding a view. Shar rdza Rinpoche says:

> Because of not searching for setting up the view, it will become liberated into its own nature. Through not having to grasp to understand this, you will be liberated from [the need for] any remedy. Through not having any cause to [engage in] meditation practice, you will be liberated from [the need for] meditating. There will be liberation from [the need to] purify any grasping, such as ordinary appearance, attachments to certain vehicles, attachment to the play of meditative experiences, and being bound by expectation [of gain] or fear [of not getting it] (112).

With respect to meditation, Shar rdza Rinpoche recommends searching for an agent meditating until it is unfindable and realized as empty (112). Until "the awakened mind-itself stays without waxing and waning, meditation practice arises in immense vastness" (113). This practice is also designed to realize the inherent emptiness of residual conceptual thought so that the practitioner isn't simply conceptualizing about the awakened mind (114). He adds, "In that awakened awareness, which is transparent and bare and is no longer covered by conceptual thought, you will establish it as an infinite vast expanse" (116-117).

With respect to conduct, the direct experience of awakening "clears away [residual] dualistic appearance" (117). With respect to fruition, emptiness practices go beyond an agent grasping for a specific outcome or fruition, and beyond expectation of a particular outcome or fear of not getting that outcome.

The next teaching is called "tying up" (*sdam pa*) in that the practitioner is so bound to the view of emptiness that "at the very moment they arise, appearances and mind are viewed as vivid, clear, and bright [lively awakened awareness]" (119). In other words, this specific teaching pertains to the quickness or immediacy of the view. Shar rdza Rinpoche says:

> The meaning of the view is like a thunderbolt falling from the sky without resistance. The meaning of meditation is like the sun arising in the sky so that all the darkness disappears, or like lightning falling. The meaning of conduct is like a flood gushing forth in some area, washing away the plants, trees, earth, and rocks. The meaning of fruition is like finding a precious wish-granting jewel that brings together and accomplishes whatever you need or desire (122).

The next and last teaching of this series is on "binding" (*chings su bcing pa*), wherein the view, meditation, conduct, and fruition are "bound moment-by-moment" to whatever immediately arises in an "unceasing" way (122).

The last section on thoroughly cutting through practice is on crossing over from the ordinary mind to the realization of awakened awareness through the "great not doing" (*byar med chen po*) (122). Shar rdza Rinpoche has distilled the pith instructions for the realization of awakening to a single essential point, namely the importance of not doing. Always right here is a limitless expanse of lucid awakened awareness. It is not possible to realize this unbounded wholeness from a partialized view. The function of conceptual thought is to delineate. Thus, each and every conceptual thought represents, by definition, a partialized view, and therefore it becomes impossible to think in any way to realize awakened awareness. The function of doing this or that is to delineate a focus for action. Thus, every instant of doing represents a partialized view, and therefore it becomes impossible to do or act in any way to realize awakened awareness. Therefore, the only antidote for conceptualizing or doing is automatic emptiness, wherein each and every momentary instant of conceptual thought and doing is automatically and immediately realized as empty upon arising. As a result, the "natural state"' (*gnas lugs*) remains freshly [absent of conceptual thought] and simply [absent of all doing]. As Shar rdza Rinpoche says, "This is called 'whatever is done becomes the practice [of emptiness of doing]'" (123). He adds, "There is no *Buddhahood* through the activity of doing. All doing is [based on] the formative [aggregate]. Therefore, all formative aggregates are impermanent. The meaning of not-doing is like space. [With respect to space], nothing is accomplished by doing or by effort, and because of that you cross over to the great freedom from doing…" (125). The nature of the meditation practice at this point is moment-by-moment to view everything that arises from the expanse of the boundless field of awareness as none other than the liveliness of awakened awareness, including every instance of thought and doing (126),… like a very powerful thoroughbred horse that automatically destroys all the vegetation under its feet as it swiftly runs (128). When the ordinary mind is cleared of all residual instances of thinking and doing, and the practitioner simply holds the view uninterruptedly, awakened awareness opens itself to itself, awakened by itself to itself, as a natural manifestation of enlightened intention (129). By holding the view of the unbounded wholeness of limitless, non-dual awareness, free of each and every instance of doing, "you never fall into going astray" (129) and the innate intelligence of awakened awareness continues to show itself to-itself, by-itself.

At this point the practitioner stabilizes the realization of awakened awareness and has attained "confidence" in the view (*gdeng*) such that it seems impossible ever to lose the realization of awakened awareness as always right here.

By-Passing

The next actual foundational practice is "by-passing" (*thod rgal*). By-passing practices are featured as the main practice in the *Heart*

Drops. Shar rdza Rinpoche begins by discussing seven ways that by-passing practice is superior to thoroughly cutting through Great Completion meditation. Thoroughly cutting through, as compared to by-passing practice, doesn't fully purify the residual substantiality of:

(1) the external world, like rocks and mountains,

(2) the physical aggregates of the body,

(3) the sense-consciousnesses,

(4) serving the welfare of sentient beings, and

(5) the subtle interferences to the full fruition as enlightenment.

(6) Then, thoroughly cutting through practice doesn't purify the sense-systems sufficiently to lead to the direct realization of the four levels of visions in by-passing; and lastly,

(7) in by-passing, as compared to thoroughly cutting through, the practitioner goes beyond all gradual levels of development to the unchanging, eternal, immense ground [of being]" (133).

The essential points of the by-passing pith instructions are introduced through a parable from the *Rig pa khu byug* [*Awakened Awareness of the Cuckoo*]:

> The king of self-knowing awakened awareness is *bodhicitta* itself. To serve the welfare of sentient beings it manifests magically as a body, which is called "the powerful bird with the extra-long beak." This bird comes out from a nest that looks like red rocks with white streaks. His lung passages are like the four [major] mothers, and four [minor] sons. Four [princes] riding on horses act to serve the welfare of sentient beings at all times. These horses, which are emanations of thoroughbreds, when they move and travel, the four great kings lift up each horse by its four legs. The four queens of the [respective] four seasons support him at the [four] sides. The four emanating winds lift him and move him. The four great rivers are the continuous flow of his merit. The four emanating fires balance the temperature. [All] have their place in the golden earth. Eight clear mirrors adorn their enlightened bodies. Three secret seed syllables manifest as their

enlightened heart-minds. The five radiant lamps are generated from the crown of his head. All the stars and planets shine from his waist. The four attendants serve him. He unceasingly serves the benefit of sentient beings and does this all the time. These are the positive qualities that come from the horses (134-135).

This parable contains forty-two distinct by-passing pith instructions. According to Shar rdza Rinpoche, the "four great kings" refers to the essential points of body, speech and mind; the essential point of the gazes to set up the by-passing visions; the essential point of the arising of the four levels of visions; and the essential point of all visions dissolving into the expanse of awakened awareness. By-passing practice begins with assuming each of three postures—the lion posture, the resting elephant posture, and the crouching *rishi* posture—to establish a direct, stable connection to the *dharmakāya, sambhogakāya,* and *nirmāṇakāya,* respectively. Speech practice refers to cutting off normal speech and remaining mute (140). Mind practice pertains to focusing the mind and the gaze in such a way as to have the direct manifestation of awakened awareness (140). The essential point of the gaze is to set up a series of specific gazes at the boundary of the eyebrow fence, so as to initiate the direct perception of the by-passing visions. The essential point of the visions as an object of focus is to look from the vast expanse through the fluid eye lamps at the boundary of the eyebrow fence, at the outer surface of the fluid eye lamps, where the visions dance on the surface of the fluid eye lamps, as if looking at images spontaneously arising in two crystal balls at once. The essential point of the winds is to inhale, inhale again to maximum capacity, hold the breath for an extended duration, and finally exhale. By holding the breath for longer and longer, the lung winds, and conceptual thought related to their activity, dissolve into the expanse of awakened awareness in such a way as to no longer obscure the direct perception of the by-passing visions (142).

The "four winds of emanation" (142) refers to the four special energy channels used in by-passing practice:

'There are four channels: the great golden *kati* channel, the white silk filament channel, the subtle coiled channel, and the crystal tube channel." According to this passage, the great golden *kati* channel, abiding in the heart, connects the heart to the center of the central channel. In the center of the heart, the heart-essence of radiant clear-light supports the complete [peaceful] assembly of the g.Yung drung [eternal swastika *Buddha* family]. [From there the channel goes to the] Brahma aperture where the wrathful deities [abide]. [The branches] of this radiant channel serve as a support for all kinds of energy drops that arise. The interior of the [second] channel is like white silk filaments. [It extends from the heart] as one channel upward, like the Tibetan vowel *e*, and divides into two channels, where one side connects to the right eye. This channel serves as a support for engaging external objects. The other side [branch channel] connects to the Brahma aperture where it serves as a support for the arising of the essence of emptiness/radiance, the great awakened awareness, absent of all conceptual thought. When this reaches full measure, it serves as a support for the arising of the five or nine energy drops that stack up in the [interior tube of the upper central channel]. The third, the subtle coiled channel, is from [the central channel at the heart down to the base] and then rises up through the center of the four *chakras* [navel, heart, throat, and crown] and joins to the left eye. It serves as a support for the arising of visions of the natural clear-light that directly arise within you. The fourth, the crystal tube channel is connected from the heart to the eyes. It serves as a support for letting the visions appear in you and subside in you (142-144).

These special channels are used to fuel the by-passing visions.

The "four fires of balancing the temperature" refers to the four lamps. Looking out from the limitless expanse of awakened awareness [the lamp of the universal ground], through the constant uninterrupted flow of lively awakened awareness through the heart lamp, and directed through the *kati* tube channel to the eyes [lamps of the soft white channels], and looking out from the fluid eye lamps just below the boundary of the eyebrow fence, that is where the visions appear on the outer surface of the fluid eye lamps (144). By holding the view of all four lamps simultaneously, "whatever visions of the radiance of awakened awareness arise are made clear as the enlightened bodies in the *Buddha*-fields" (144). These visions are perceived from the perspective of non-duality, not as "out there" but as generated from internal light. The visions arise from the expanse of groundless ground, "the golden earth" (147), as the manifestation of lively awakened awareness.

The "four great rivers" (147) refers to the flow of the four levels of visions. The visions first appear at the eyebrow fence as active energy drops, like boiling water, like spheres or cells under a microscope, like filaments and threads, and like splashes of certain colors. They arise on the surface of the fluid eye lamps like reflections in a mirror (148). At first "these [visions] arise, either clear or clouded" (148). If the first level of visions fails to appear, the practitioner engages in sun gazing in the early morning or late afternoon before the sun is too strong. He or she focuses at the boundary of the eyebrow fence in the daytime with the sun at his or her back, or looking at the sun in front with a protective cloth covering the eyes [protecting them] from being damaged by the sun. Then, a cascade of colored lights, energy drops, and filaments will dance on the surface of the fluid eye lamps.

The second level of visions is the proliferation of visions in the form of simple patterns and shapes, and a complete array of colored lights. These visions are no longer limited to being perceived at the boundary of the eyebrow fence (150) but now fill the entire field of awareness. They are much bigger in size. Shar rdza Rinpoche says:

> At times the visions proliferate, and the expanse and awakened awareness separate from the eyebrow boundary. The five lights of the five primordial wisdoms come [straight] upwards [from the eyebrow boundary], like spokes and squares, or in the form of felt. Sometimes the visions seem as large as a country. There are visions of colors. [Visions] in the form of eyes in a net, a web, a bouquet of flowers, and the symbols of the *Buddha* families or their celestial palaces. These are the visions of [various] shapes. This is called "the development of light from space." These visions are also like *stupas*, hooks, tridents, arrows, spearheads, and so forth (150-151).

The energy drops start out about the size of a pea but now grow in size to the size of a shield (151).

The transition to the third level of visions is marked by the perception that the energy drops gradually slow down and eventually become stationary. Shar rdza Rinpoche says, "They quickly fly by like a bird; or they seem to run like a deer through the rock faces of the mountains; or then they move very slowly like the [mythical creature, the] *sharana* [like a slowly crawling slug]. Finally, they move very slowly, much like a honey bee hovering over a flower" (152). By looking into these stationary energy drops, much like shearing off the top of an egg shell, entire *Buddha*-fields become manifest. Each single energy drop is like a computer chip that contains the entire world of the *sambhogakāya Buddha*-fields. Because at this third level the entire field of visions of the *Buddha*-fields appears as spontaneously present, it is described in the parable as "all the stars and planets" appearing all at once (152). All that is required at this level is to hold the view uninterruptedly. Shar rdza Rinpoche says, "At the time of seeing the embodiment of enlightenment, the essential point for completing that is to look unchangingly at its radiance" (153). At this level, the visions are said to "reach full measure...you reach the fruition...the truth of the path of the *maṇḍala* of the enlightened completion bodies" (153).

As a result, the eighty-three positive qualities of an enlightened *Buddha* mind become manifest. Furthermore, the five primordial wisdoms merge as spontaneously present. This is symbolized in the parable as five colored lights emerging from the crown (155). Furthermore, the first signs of the three-fold embodiment of enlightenment become manifest. This is symbolized in the parable as the "three secret seed-syllables" (157). This is the onset of path enlightenment (158).

At the fourth level, the visions wind down and cease altogether. This is sometimes referred to as the exhaustion of the visions in the *dharmadhātu* (158). Shar rdza Rinpoche says, "The solidness of the external objects and the physical body have reached full measure and become exhausted...[all] subtle karmic seeds of habitual karmic tendencies become exhausted" (159). At this level, the entire world and the internal landscape of the physical body is perceived as light, conceptual thought as light-rays, and sound as the ultimate sound of lively awakened awareness. These are the three resultant pure visions—light, light-rays, and ultimate sound.

As a consequence of realizing this fourth level of by-passing visions the practitioner reaches fruition enlightenment. There are "two attainments"—freedom from future rebirths in *saṁsāra* and great consciousness-transference (160).

Great and Standard Consciousness-Transference

The last section of the *Heart Drops* is on great consciousness-transference. This refers to the final outcome of by-passing practice in Bon Great Completion meditation, namely dissolving all residual substantiality of the physical body until the physical body is entirely reduced to pure rainbow light. This is called "rainbow body" (*ja lus*). Shar rdza Rinpoche says:

> This is called "the arising of the enlightened embodiment of the Great Consciousness-Transference [Rainbow Body]." Then, you qualify for the same status of the first twenty-four masters of the rainbow body [awareness-holder lineage]. This kind of body-holder is such that others with impure eyes see it [your body] as substantial, but to you, your body also appears transparent. In an instant, if you want, you could make your body invisible [to others] (160).

In this manner the practitioner attains the status of the lineage of the twenty-four Bon awareness-holders of the rainbow body lineage. The parable describes the "four queens of the four seasons" (162). The first queen refers to the "three immovable bases," namely holding an immovable body posture, an immovable gaze, and an immovable mind on the view (162).

The second queen refers to the "three stabilities," namely the stability of the physical body posture, the stability of the winds, through which conceptual thought subsides, and the stability of the visions, through which the direct perception of the *Buddha*-fields becomes manifest.

Through these stabilization practices many signs of meditative progress occur (163). For example, a clear sign of integrating these realizations at the deepest levels of mind is that dreams completely cease (as a consequence of the exhaustion of the ripening of habitual karmic propensities), and deep sleep is no longer an unconscious state but is characterized by the experience of awakening throughout deep sleep, as the clear-light of deep sleep (166).

The third queen refers to the "four attainments" (167) through which "all conditions arise as friends to the visions...the body no longer appears as solid but as clear-light...[and the] conceptual mind subsides in the expanse."

The fourth queen refers to the "four confidences" (167), which refers to: being beyond all expectation of an outcome; being beyond fear of not getting that outcome; being confident of no longer falling into future lower rebirths; and no longer falling back into *saṁsāra* (167).

Finally, the "four servants" in the *Cuckoo* parable refers to the development of four kinds of sublime knowledge that support the realizations.

The *Heart Drops* contains a final section on standard consciousness-transference for "those of middling capacity" who, not being of best capacity, are unlikely to achieve the rainbow body through great consciousness-transference practice at the time of dying. Once the practitioner of middling capacity recognizes the signs, he or she is dying, he or she must go to a quiet place to prepare to practice during the dying process. Shar rdza Rinpoche says:

> A person of best capacity is like a small child who doesn't care about dying or not dying. They don't need these instructions. A person of middling capacity dies like a dog. Out of them the best are not harmed by objects and conditions, like [dying] on the road, a city, or crowded cross-road. Those of middling middling capacity go to a cave, mountain, or desolate valley, or a place where they can't be seen. Those of lesser middling capacity are like a king dying. When he gets sick [attendants] use medicine and perform rituals. When dying, he is surrounded by relatives and friends. They shed tears. With his final suffering words he gives his last testament as he dies. Even after he dies, they per-

form rituals: seven-day rituals, funerary rites, and so forth. The way of dying like this is the sign of not having the confidence of the practice of Great Completion (170).

Such practitioners must then remember their previous instructions about and direct realization of awakened awareness as they transition into the dying process (172). Next, the practitioner widens and re-opens the upper central channel as done some years ago in standard consciousness-transference practice. The practitioner repeatedly utters *"HIG"* while imagining a thumb-sized seed-syllable pushing its way progressively up the upper central channel to widen and re-open this passageway from the heart to the crown. In the dying process itself, each of the elements dissolve, one-by-one —earth, then water, then fire, then wind, then space. What remains is a direct experience of "clear-light, like a cloudless sky" (174). The practitioner previously familiar with the direct realization of awakened awareness during his or her previous lifetime is highly likely to recognize this clear-light of dying at this phase of the dying process, and with such realization immediately becomes a *Buddha*.

If the practitioner fails to recognize the clear-light of dying during the dying process, and through that become liberated, he or she enters the *bardo* of *dharmadhātu*. This *bardo* is essentially a sound and light show with a series of visions much like the four levels of by-passing visions. If the practitioner recognizes these visions as self-appearing, non-dual, and empty pure light, he or she becomes liberated in the *bardo* of *dharmadhātu* as a fully enlightened *Buddha* in awakened *dharmakāya* space wherein the practitioner remains "in a state of g.Yung drung [eternal] Bon" (179).

It is extremely important that the practitioner remember the pith instructions. This entails remembering the specific pith instruction given by your lama, remembering the right view, and remembering the after-death visions as the non-dual self-arising liveliness of awakened awareness (180). Those at risk to forget these vital instructions can intentionally propel the indestructible essence from its resting place in the central channel after death and out the Brahma aperture. The result is consciousness-transference to the emanating *Buddha*-fields. Shar rdza Rinpoche says:

At this point in time, awakened awareness is propelled like a shooting star, imagining it like a ball of light coming out from the Brahma aperture. At this point in time, [it is important] to remember these [innate emanating] *Buddha*-fields. Imagine awakened awareness in the form of a [seed-syllable] *A* (183) and put in the effort to propel [your mind] carefully again and again into the enlightened heart-mind of the principle [*Buddha*] of that realm (182-183).

The specific *Buddha*-field that becomes evident depends on the practitioner's natural disposition (184).

This completes the introductory discussion of the *Heart Drops*.

Herein is the Explanatory Practical Guide on the Clear-Light of the Stages of the Bon Dzogchen Path Known as

"Heart Drops of Kuntuzangpo"

Written by
Shardza Tashi Gyaltsen
(1859 – 1934)

Translated by
Geshe Sonam Gurung and Daniel P. Brown, Ph.D.

Under the Guidance of
H.H. the 33rd Menri Trizin

1. This text was originally translated into English by Lopon Tenzin Namdak as *Heart Drops of Dharmakāya*, Ithaca, NY: Snow Lion, 1993. That translation was based on lectures he gave on the text to a small group of Western students in Nepal in 1991. However, that translation, based on live lectures, is not a line-by-line translation of the original Tibetan text, and many quoted passages from other texts were omitted. Therefore, we have made this new, line-by-line, complete translation available here. This new translation also contains a translation of technical terms familiar to our students.

(78) This is the explanatory practice guide on the clear-light of the stages of the Great Completion path known as "*Heart Drops of Kun tu bZang po.*"

Homage to gShen lha 'Od dkar, who illuminated self-occurring awakened awareness!

The natural state of *dharmakāya* has a nature that is inconceivable like the expanse of space. The elaboration of its being substantial or having [definable] characteristics does not need to be abandoned in this primordially non-existing, unadulterated state because it is [already] endowed with the best of what is continuously and spontaneously accomplished, namely the embodiment of enlightenment and the primordial wisdoms. All [sentient beings] have primordially directly manifested this realization as the play of my own mind, like a lotus [manifesting spontaneously] in a lake. From a state immovable from this natural state, the play of the liveliness of the visions directly arises. This is the Lord who shows the *maṇḍala's* array of its magical emanations as the ten completions of unchanging eternal Bon (79) and its inconceivable, indeterminate, peaceful and wrathful emanations. The queen, the bearer of white light, helps me to give the best of the teachings in my heart. The condition of Kun tu bZang po is this same non-duality. By the *samādhi* endowed with the four liberations, the endpoint, the clear-light of *dharmakāya*, becomes directly manifest, along with the unchanging primordial wisdom of the *sambhogakāya*. Extending to the end of space is the great hero, who has no fear of the end of life. May Dran pa Nam mkha' protect me thereafter at all times in my future lives. Who, other than he, could have investigated with his stainless intelligence, omniscience, and divine eyes (80) the ultimate truth of the profound vast *tantra* [teachings], whose nature is like an ocean of space, and is difficult [for most] to realize?

In that case, having been encouraged by those virtuous ones with supreme aspiration, faith, and diligence, I should teach this profound path to those fortunate ones for them to take into their crowns [i.e., take it with respect]. Glorious Kun tu bZang po, who completed authentic *Buddhahood* in the pure celestial palaces spontaneously present in the primordial expanse, through profound enlightened intention taught this to immeasurable followers. His enlightened intention never moves from the expanse of *dharmadhātu*, and the five *Buddhas* are none other than himself, and the fruition of that is the ultimate nature of Great Completion and the *tantras*, the best of all Bon teachings. Its vastness is immeasurable, innumerable, and countless. There are forty-two branches of *tantric* teachings and three series of teachings, but these are not the best of these heart-essence [teachings]. These here come [directly] from those (81) endowed with limitless pith instructions.

Once again, for those endowed with fortunate karma, here are the skillful means to directly bring about complete *Buddhahood*. These profound teachings about the quick path of clear-light Great Completion have three divisions. Those ones of the highest capacity group connect to the expanse of pure universal ground [in this very lifetime]. Those of middling capacity become enlightened in the after-death *bardos*. Those of lesser capacity give up their last breath in the innate *Buddha*-fields of the *nirmāṇakāyas*. There are specific skillful means for each [group].

This text pertains to the first [highest capacity practitioner] for which there are two divisions—the preliminary stages and the practice of the essential points of the actual foundational practices.

1.0 Preliminaries 81

The first [the preliminary practices] has two divisions:

(1) stopping engagement in *saṁsāra* through the three gateways, by distinguishing *saṁsāra* and *nirvāṇa*; and

(2) reversing attachment to the body and mind as objects by training the three gateways—body, speech, and mind.

1.1 Distinguishing Between Saṁsāra and Nirvāṇa 81

The first has two divisions—external and internal.

1.1.1 External Practices 81

As for the first, distinguishing [saṁsāra and nirvāṇa], Master Dran pa Nam mkha' said, "Consider that all the suffering behaviors of the six classes of beings are experienced in your own mind-stream. Do the activities of the physical body by moving, running, standing, sitting (82). Make the sounds of speech intensely. Through that, cut the thread of activities that cause fatigue. Do this again and again, and you will reach clarity about these essential points." According to this passage, go to a [quiet] place where you do not see or sense any people wandering or going. Make a dough offering to the [local] spirits. Promise them [you are practicing] and won't engage in shameless activities or be angry.

To distinguish saṁsāra and nirvāṇa via the three gateways, have them serve the purpose of all sentient beings. Thereafter, generate a mind that thinks you won't come again into saṁsāra in the future. Then [imagine] the physical body being naked and do [imitations of] the bodily activities of each of the respective six realms and all of the six classes of beings there—the [lower] hell realm beings, hungry ghosts, and animals are liberated [over time] by ascending [from the lower realms], and the [higher] human, god, and demi-god realm beings descend [from the upper realms] and gradually fall [from those realms]. Likewise, make all sorts of sounds [of these respective sentient beings] through speaking. Generate conceptual thoughts and recollections of mind and practice [these] as liveliness.

As was previously said, "Do imitations of the peaceful and wrathful deities' bodies. Say whatever you remember of the deities' mantras by reciting them. Your mind is taken to be the divine pride of your *yi dam* [tutelary deity] or the [*maṇḍala*] deities" (83). According to this passage, [imagine] how sTon pa g.Shen rab in 'Ol gling taught the eternal *bodhisattvas* and turned the stages of three wheels of Bon, and how the three roots of these immortal secret *mantra* teachings were entrusted to the awareness-holders of the gods, *Nāgas*, and humans [respectively]. The way Kun tu bZang po taught Great Completion teachings to the *Sugatas* of the five *Buddha* families was at the site of the 'Og Min [*Buddha*-fields]. Those [teachings] descended gradually, and eventually were integrated into their mind-streams. Then, these became the way to spontaneously dissolve the gateways of *saṁsāra*, the way to dissolve the spontaneous visions in the original purity of the expanse, and the way the array of the spontaneous *Buddha*-fields in their original purity over and over served the benefit of beings. [To use these teachings] let go of all appearances and hold the mind without any reference point. The period of these [practices] is three, two, or one month.

In the *gSer thur* [*Golden Spoon*] it says, "The positive qualities come in one month." According to this passage, the reason is that your instantaneous [ordinary] mind is the root of all *saṁsāra* and *nirvāṇa*. Therefore, by imitating the conduct of all the beings in the six classes of beings by these intense means and acting accordingly, find the agent [who is doing this conduct]. Through that, you will know that it depends on the mind (84) and that the agent is categorized as within the mind. Through knowing that, the ways [each of] the six classes of beings appear at this time are merely understood as the manifestations of the mind. Through knowing that, you will come to know the essence of the mind as being emptiness, and stop the cause of *saṁsāra*. Through stopping that, you will come to know the fruition of having stopped *saṁsāra* thereafter, [namely] not engaging in *saṁsāra*. In the *Don rgyud* [*Tantra of Truth*] it says, "Thereafter, you will not return to *saṁsāra*."

According to this passage, the second distinction is internal.

1.1.2 Internal Practices 84

These are the instructions from the *Rigs drug rang sbyong* [*Self-Purification of the Six Realms*]. Practice the meditation as it is described there.

1.2 Reversing Attachment to the Body and Mind as Objects by Training the Three Gateways—Body, Speech, and Mind 84

There are three divisions to training with the three gateways.

1.2.1 Body Practice 84

First, are the body practices. In the *gSer thur* [*Golden Spoon*] it says, "The body is set up according to the instructions on the *vajra*. The eyeballs focus in space without distraction. The [estimated] amount of time [to complete the practice] is three and a half days. The resultant positive qualities are occasional or lasting." According to this passage, stand up and place the soles of both feet together with the knees spread out. Forcibly make the torso upright. Both hands make the prayer position just above [the head] but not touching the crown, with the elbows extended out. The neck is slightly bent toward the chest (85). Having done that, hold the physical body [this way] and stay as long as you are able, and meditate on it [the elbows and hands in prayer position] as if it were a three-pointed *vajra*, with flames of fire. When you are unable to hold the breath any longer, fall down backwards, and discontinue by exhaling "*HA*." Repeat this again and again.

There are three reasons it is set up like this. The standard [reason] is that it purifies the obscurations that bring fatigue to the body. The special [reason] is that because [negative spirits] see the flames of fire from the *vajra* body, it removes harmful influences and calms the hindrances. Ultimately, it directly stops attachment to the physical body. You will have accomplished the enlightened *nirmāṇakāya* body. In the *Yab sras don rgyud* [*Tantra of Ultimate Truth of Father and Son*] it says, "By practicing over and over again you will purify [all the] ordinary obscurations of the physical body. Hindrances will become calm and you will directly stop attachment to the physical body. Ultimately, you will manifest and become inseparable from the *nirmāṇakāyas*."

1.2.2 **Speech Practice** 85

1.2.2.1 **Sealing1 Speech** 85

In order to illuminate the speech practice, the *rGyud kyi rgyal po* [*King of Tantra*] says, "To stay, utter the sound '*HUNG*'." Of [the four practices]—sealing, skillful practice, practicing pliancy, and establishing the path—bring the benefits to mind of your having practiced like this." According to this passage, four types of [speech] practices have been illuminated. The first, sealing, has three subdivisions. The etymology [of sealing] (86): the appearance to you of the impure mind is [in the form of] the physical body. The seed-syllable that stays in the form of a *HUNG* [symbolizes] the essence of primordial wisdom, which is the

---

1. *rgyas gdab*: "sealing."

secret enlightened heart-mind of the *Buddha*. Sealing the clouds as pure visions is called "sealing."

Second, there are two practices [of sealing]—external and internal.

1.2.2.1.1 **External** 86

With respect to external appearances, sealing [begins with] setting up the essential body-points, as previously described, endowed with being cross-legged, etc. The eyes focus on the surrounding space. Imagine a blue *HUNG* in the heart. Express the sound "*HUNG HUNG HUNG*" [repeatedly] long and slow, [and at the same time imagine] that from the *HUNG* in the heart innumerable, subtle *HUNG*s emanate and then come out from the right nostril. Then, imagine that all stable external appearances of the container and all moving events as the contents [of the mind] transform into splendorous *HUNG*s. Then, by imagining that all three—winds, mind, and appearance—mix into one, your mind arises in the form of a [seed-syllable] *HUNG*. The sound of wind is made by the sound of *HUNG*. Imagine that [all external] appearances exist as naturally innate *HUNG*s.

1.2.2.1.2 **Internal** 86

Second, is sealing internally with respect to the physical aggregates [of the body]. Through expressing a short [fast rhythm], "*HUNG HUNG*," internally imagine that all the outside *HUNG*s enter back through the left nostril, and, having returned to the inside of interior space [of the body], as a result all the flesh and blood inside this [body] (87) [transforms into *HUNG*s and] becomes insubstantial.

Then, imagine that everything outside and inside the physical body becomes filled and overflowing with *HUNG*s.

1.2.2.1.3 **The Purpose of Sealing** 87

Third, the purpose [of sealing] is that [all] appearing objects without inherent existence become liberated. The elements of the physical body become purified. Being insubstantial and without outflows they also become liberated. The full measure of mastery is described in the *gSer zhun* [*Refined Gold*] where it says, "[As signs of progress] all external appearances [spontaneously] arise as the splendor of the *HUNG*s, as do the physical aggregates [of the body] internally. The agent that considers them solid is also sealed as *HUNG*s. Sealing leads to the signs of genuine mastery."

1.2.2.2 Skillful[2] Practice 87

Second, skillful practice has three divisions. The etymology of skillful practice is such that the [seemingly solid] appearances that appear as your own mind are dismantled by the mind's skill, so it is called "skillful practice." Practicing the meditation has two divisions—external and internal practice.

1.2.2.2.1 External 87

Through expressing intensely and fiercely the sounds "*HUNG HUNG HUNG*," imagine that from this awakened awareness *HUNG*, [in the center of the heart, innumerable] dark blue *HUNG*s emanate with their full force like lightning bolts, or like the full intensity of a cosmic fire, or like the full sharpness of [the arrows of] a weapon wheel, or like the swift flash of lightning [come out from the right nostril]. After many of these [*HUNG*s] erupt, imagine all the [external] appearances, like mountains and houses that arise, as these [appearances that previously served as] obstacles are touched [by the *HUNG*s], all of them here, and all of them there, are also pierced [and destroyed] so as to become insubstantial and permeable.

1.2.2.2.2 Internal 88

Second, practice with the internal aggregates: Through expressing the sound "*HUNG HUNG*" [repeatedly], imagine *HUNG*s the size of one finger span with a characteristic blue color, like the color lapis lazuli [come back through the left nostril]. These [*HUNG*s] have a characteristic force, much like thunderbolts of lightning. These also have a characteristic heat [and burn] the objects of awareness, much like being in the midst of a cosmic fire. They also have a characteristic of destroying, much like a typical *vajra* [or diamond]. Having these four characteris-

---

2. *rtsal shyong ba*: "skillful practice."

tics, imagine [the *HUNG*s] piercing through all external objects and then [also piercing] everything inside [the body, with the mind] without a fixation point, and thereby purifying even the smallest particles [of the physical body and external world].

1.2.2.2.3 The Purpose of Skillful Practice 88

Third, the purposes are to purify all appearances as not truly existent, to calm all illnesses and harmful influences, and to make the [residual] physical body dissolve into clear-light. The full measure of mastery is described in the *gSer zhun* [*Refined Gold*] where it says, "[As signs of progress] through skillful practice on appearances, meditative experience arises of all appearances dissolving. The physical aggregates [of the body], and the elements that arise also appear like [an insubstantial] net. These are the signs of mastery of skillful practice."

1.2.2.3 Practicing Pliancy³ 88

Third, pliancy has three divisions. First, the etymology of pliancy is that the mind in-and-by-itself is brought under control, and because of that it is called "pliancy." Second, is skillful means to practice meditation.

1.2.2.3.1 External 89

Place a long object to support concentration in front of yourself, such as a stick. Through expressing a long pleasant sound, "*HUNG HUNG*," many *HUNG*s come out from the *HUNG* in the heart like a string of rosary beads [and leave the body through the nostrils] and go to the base of the [stick], the object to support concentration. They gradually wrap around the stick, and then they reach the top, and these *HUNG*s as before [face you] in front. Then, focus the mind on settling on this and staying on it, and sing a song slowly of *HUNG*s.

1.2.2.3.2 Internal 89

Then bring [the *HUNG*s] slowly back to the [*HUNG* in the] heart. If conceptual thought rises up, imagine that the first *HUNG* dissolves into the next *HUNG* and then dissolves into the *HUNG* in the heart at the end.

---

3. *mnyen btsal*: "pliancy."

1.2.2.3.3 **Purpose** 89

Third, the purpose is that by practicing over and over again, by bringing the vicissitudes of external [appearances] and internal conceptual thoughts into the path in the mind, you will attain the completely purified positive qualities and you are able to transform these into anything you focus on.

1.2.2.4 **Engaging as Path**[4] 89

Fourth, engaging as path has three divisions.

1.2.2.4.1 **Etymology** 89

The etymology is that by having trained with the three—[external] object, physical body, and mind—you put them in their right way as innate clear-light and so this is called "engaging them as the path."

1.2.2.4.2 **The Skillful Means of Practicing the Meditation** 89

Second, the skillful means of practicing the meditation is to imagine your own body, wind [speech], and mind as a single blue *HUNG* (90) [the size of] a forearm's length. Then numerous *HUNG*s travel like insects being carried here and being carried there to places seen like mountains and the countryside, and then moving to places never seen, and additionally, to limitless mountains and valleys. Coordinate the gentle expression of the *HUNG* with the way the mind moves [back and forth and in front]. Then, stop [the *HUNG*s] with the sound *"PHAT,"* set up the mind without reference point, and recognize the primordial state. Again, express *"HUNG HUNG"* continuously, and imagine shooting these *HUNG*s, like a skilled archer shooting an arrow, going directly to the pure *Buddha*-fields like 'Ol mo'i gLing and the eastern Shar phyogs mngon dga' ba [*Buddha*-field] and so forth, and then set up the mind without reference point to cross over.

Through that, you will purify the habitual karmic tendencies associated with objects, and conceptual thought will stop by its own power. Then, you will generate the meditative experiences of bliss, luminosity, and stillness. In the *gSer zhun* [*Refined Gold*] it says, "By practicing pliancy,

---

4. *lam gzhug*: "engaging as path."

engaging as path, and so forth, when you let the mind go, it goes, and when you focus, it stays with stability. If the influence of dualistic thought elaboration occurs, it is the sign of not having pliancy or not engaging it as the path (91). According to this passage, practice the meditation until the signs reach full measure.

1.2.2.4.3 The Purpose 91

The purpose of practicing with sound is that you purify all obscurations of speech and accomplish the *sambhogakāya*. In the *Don rgyud* [*Tantra of Ultimate Truth of Father and Son*] it says, "Purify the vices and calm the hindrances of speech. Having directly stopped all attachment of speech, ultimately these become inseparable from the *sambhogakāya*." So it is said.

1.2.3 Mind Practice 91

Third, mind practice has two divisions:

(1) the nine skillful means to determine the concentrated mind as awakened mind-itself, and

(2) cutting the root of the mind's basis in coming, staying, and going.

1.2.3.1 The Nine Skillful Means to Determine Mind as Awakened Mind-Itself 91

First, it says in the *gSer gyi lung non che ba* [*Great Subduers of the Golden Prophesies*], "Those endowed with the right karmic connection make a search into the emptiness of their own minds using the nine ways to establish these as mere designations without [substantiality]. These nine ways are:

(1) examine and search your own mind as empty;

(2) examine and search into appearances;

(3) examine and search appearances as without inherent nature;

(4) examine and search appearance/emptiness and transcending all limit;

(5) examine and search as existing;

(6) examine and search as non-existing;

(7) examine and search as not existing as either;

(8) examine and search into the basis; and

(9) search the basis as never lost and without [substantiality]. There is no searching and no not-searching. These are mere designations" (92).

According to this passage, if you have not yet realized the awakened mind-itself, it has been said that it [mind] should be searched for [until it becomes unfindable].

1.2.3.1.1 Examine and Search Your Own Mind as Empty 92

The first of these is as follows. Assume the five-fold body posture. Then, examine the source of thoughts in your own mind, whether they exist or do not exist as substantial, or whether they have definable characteristics. [Examine it] by turning inwardly. Through that, there is nothing whatsoever to the object to be examined, nor the agent doing the examining. It becomes totally empty like space. Take hold of this unborn essence of the mind.

1.2.3.1.2 Examine and Search Into Appearances 92

Second, regarding whatever does not exist, and the agent that makes it not exist: [search whether it] does exist or does not exist. Through examining it not existing, is it eliminated or destroyed? Is there an antidote that destroys it? Even if you consider it improper to stop it, the essence it has is clear, and becomes more and more clear, more and more awake, and more and more vivid [as you examine it]. Take hold of the mind as having inherent unobstructedness.

1.2.3.1.3 Examine and Search Appearances as Without Inherent Nature 92

Third, by having examined it like this, [you realize] this mind is empty and is without substantiality or [definable] characteristics. It arises as clarity, as the very primordial wisdom itself, free of obscurations. It is [the inseparable pair] clarity/emptiness, beyond all limitations. The truth of this experience is without such a name (93). Take hold of the mind that is without characteristics and is non-dual.

1.2.3.1.4 Examine and Search Appearance/Emptiness as Transcending All Limits 93

Fourth, these [external] appearances primordially have no independent existence. So, at this point in time, those appearances taken as real are just deluded appearances, and are not genuinely true. For example, they are like the substance in a dream. In the case that they seem to exist as real, by dismantling the smallest particles [of substantiality by searching into it], they dissolve into space thereafter. [If you think] it should exist as real, it is without any [substantial] existence. With respect to whatever appears, if you examine it like this, it will arise as unreal, much like the experience of an illusion. Take hold of the mind as unobstructed play.

1.2.3.1.5 Examine and Search as Existing 93

Fifth, if the mind does not exist, where do appearances come from and to whom do they appear? Who is the agent of these appearances? Who is it that proclaims its name? Who is it that experiences the happiness or misery? Because everything that exists is made by mind, [that is why] it [mind seems to] exist. It never was not existing. Because [the mind seems to] exist, everything seems to have existence. Nothing exists [apart from mind], not even the smallest particle of something changing into something else. Earth is not earth [but is mind]. Stone is not stone [but is mind]. Appearances are not appearances [but are mind]. These exist as the deluded appearances of the mind. Realizing this as such, take hold of the mind as the king, the agent of everything.

1.2.3.1.6 Examine and Search as Non-Existing 93

Sixth, if the mind were to exist, then it would be possible for it to directly appear, yet it does not appear [like this]. Therefore, it does not exist. If it exists, it is not something that is directly manifest (94), so must not exist. This very thing [the mind] does not exist in the three times, so does it exist in-itself? The essence of this does not exist, but awakened awareness exists. With respect to awakened awareness, it cannot be described whatsoever by any names, words, or letters, and cannot be defined. Even if you [try to] define it, you can't go to it. It is not something you can go to. Having examined it like this, your realization becomes like a mute person who has tasted molasses [and can't describe it to others]. Take hold of the mind as thoughtless and expressionless.

1.2.3.1.7 Examine and Search as Not Existing as Either 94

Seventh, whether the mind were to exist or not exist, [with respect to either of these views] it does not exist as real. It not existing also does not exist, because there is no means to abandon it. Both existing and not existing do not exist, and both do not, not exist. When nothing whatsoever can be asserted about it, it is beyond being something that can be established [as real]. Having examined it like this, when one side [of the extreme position] is blocked by the other [position], then it is free from all extremes. Your realization of this extraordinary truth comes through taking hold of the mind as immense limitlessness.

1.2.3.1.8 Examining and Searching Into the Basis 94

Eighth, but then what can you say about this mind of yours by examining it? As was previously said, "The non-conceptual mind cannot be examined as an object of conceptual thought." According to this passage, by there being [no basis] to thought, giving a name to thought ends. It is like trying to illustrate [the mind] with an example, and being unable to illustrate it (95). In the case that you have continuously examined it by looking back to [its source] again, and having examined it, having the experience [of emptiness], still your realization is not something that has name or meaning. Take hold of the mind that is nameless and beyond thought.

1.2.3.1.9 Search the Basis as Never Lost and as Without [Substantiality] 95

Ninth, because the awakened mind-itself is without inherent nature, even if you search for it, there is no basis to find it. If you do not search, too, it is never lost and it never vanishes. Primordially it exists within you. It stays within you. It exists by itself within you. Is it possible that you could lose yourself? By your searching in yourself what can be found? Then, with respect to this awakened mind-itself, because it is without inherent nature, there is no designation of searching or not searching.

[Yet], it is never separated from you in the three times.

In the *De nyid* [*Suchness*] it says, "Neither coming nor going, it exists as the primordial expanse. Never lost, never separated, it exists primordially within you. Never having searched. Never searching. There is no designation as 'searcher.' [Affirm that] it arises as the unchanging enlightened body, without obscuration, as primordial wisdom. By looking, you will come to see your own true face. There is no other cause of seeing this whatsoever." According to this passage, you come to the realization that this awakened mind-itself exists primordially as self-occurring in you (96). Take hold of the mind that is effortless, spontaneous presence.

Therefore, there are no nine minds, but from [the perspective] of its aspects, by examining and searching like this, you will have cut off its very root and basis, so as to come to the realization of awakened mind-itself, the one great interconnected sphere of ultimate reality, [and will have] the bare realization of transparent awakened awareness as the *dharmakāya*.

1.2.3.2 The Basis of Mind in Coming, Staying, and Going 96

1.2.3.2.1 Coming 96

Second, having made a determination about transparent awakened awareness as being beyond all conceptualization accordingly, and having cut off the root and basis of [thought] elaboration in the mind, [seeing it as] the liveliness of awakened awareness, thereafter examine the three—coming, staying, and going—in the mind. In the *gSer gyi thur ma'i rgyud* [*Golden Spoon*] it says, "Examine the three—coming, staying, and going—in the mind. Through this examination there is nothing found but empty essence. What is left is without reference point, just alert wonder." According to this passage, examine its origin the very first moment [a thought] is coming, and [examine] the agent of its coming. In the instant that a thought arises in the mind, when it comes, where does it come from? If [you think] it comes from inside as something substantially existing, or [you think it] comes from inside as empty and non-existing, [then] if it were to come from the inside as substantially existing, when it comes, [search to see] can you find it thereafter in external stones, mountains, rocks, houses? Inside your own body, and so forth? Having destroyed even the very smallest particles of substantiality of each and every appearance (97) by searching, is there any [source of] coming that could be found? If you think [the source of] coming is inside of empty space, then no coming can be found. Suppose it is empty like space. Having searched for its origin in the four elements in space, you will realize that you can't find it. By examining it accordingly, you will not find its origin. If you consider the agent that knows this coming, it arises suddenly from space much like a great wind [in the atmosphere].

Well then, when you focus directly on the agent that knows this coming to recognize it, you should examine if it exists like this: does it exist as substantial; does it exist as having color; does it exist as one or many, and so forth? See if you can find the agent by having examined and searched. Then, look back to the mind that is searching, and through looking [into this searching mind, see that there] is nothing whatsoever to find. Then, the origin and the agent coming are [both] without dualistic grasping of appearing objects. This mind is without support, very much beyond reflections and expressions. [Realizing this], you will remain astonished.

At this point in time on the path, the view becomes limitless. At the time of the fruition it is called "unborn *dharmakāya*." As it was said in the *rdzogs chen Don rgyud* [*Tantra of Ultimate Truth of Father and Son*] (98), "The essence of the mind is without any origin of coming. In a state of self-occurring emptiness, it is bright and vivid. The view is said to be bare, without looking. Free of [conceptual] elaboration[5] it is pointed out to be *dharmakāya*." So it is said.

1.2.3.2.2 Staying 98

Second, examining the basis of staying and the agent of staying is as follows: If you think this so-called "mind" exists within you right now, does it stay anywhere? Everything that tends toward being substantial [by examining it] destroys even the smallest particles [of substantiality], and when these dissolve into space, what seems to exist does not stay. It is without any basis to its staying. If you become aware of the agent of staying, you should identify that [as insubstantial] until it becomes more

---

5. Spelling mistake: Text has *thal*. It should be *'bral*.

and more clear, and more and more awake. By identifying that, come to know both the basis of staying and the agent of staying as not inherently existing. Looking out there, there is [only] emptiness and openness. Looking here there is transparency. [Looking] straight ahead, it is uninterrupted self-clarity and self-brightness. At the time of the path, it is self-clarity meditation. The time of fruition is the unobstructed *sambhogakāya*. Previously, it was said, "By looking to find the object of staying, it stays as self-clarity and self-brightness. This is pointed out as the *sambhogakāya*." So it is said (99).

1.2.3.2.3 Going 99

Third, examining the basis of going and the agent of going is as follows: when thought suddenly arises in the mind and then disappears, by examining what makes it go, and wherever it seems to go, at first you won't find any basis to its coming, and lastly you won't find any basis to its going. If you seem to find it, you should know the agent of going accordingly, and so forth. Therefore, when you examine it like this, it isn't like that, and it fades. It is purified through being self-purified. Delusion need not be abandoned. Liberation need not be taken up. In being self-arising/self-liberated, its emptiness becomes more and more purified. This is called "at the time of [taking up] the path, practicing without a trace." At the time of the fruition, it is called "non-dual *nirmāṇakāya*." In the *De nyid* [*Suchness*] it says, "By looking nakedly wherever conceptual thought and the mind goes, it is like a fresh breeze that disappears in its own way. Self-liberation is being liberated as insubstantial and naked. Without grasping, you are meeting your own face as the *nirmāṇakāya*." According to this passage, you might take this so-called "mind" to be self-grasping an "I", but through examining the three—coming, staying, and going—you will determine that it does not exist (100). This is called "the collapse of the house of the mind." However and whenever you reach this [realization], you reach the awakened mind-itself beyond coming and going, selflessness, primordial emptiness, immense limitlessness. Then, there is no [need to] set it up [the mind] with conceptual thought, or to have an agent that sets it up. This is called "the natural, innate disposition of Great Completion, primordial clear-light itself, the ultimate truth becomes directly manifest naked and bare."

The purpose of training the mind is described in the *sKu gsum Don rgyud* [*Tantra of Ultimate Truth of the Threefold Embodiment of Enlightenment*] where it says, "By this, purify the sins and obscurations of the mind. Calm the hindrances, and directly turn back attachment regarding the sense-mind. In the end you will directly become inseparable from non-duality and the *dharmakāya*." So it is said.

2.0 Actual Foundational Practices 100

The second section on the essential points of the meditation practice of the actual foundational practices has two divisions.

2.1 Methods for Entering the Gateway of the Path 100

First, are the methods for entering the gateway of the path and its actual foundational practices, and for entering the great *maṇḍala* through the gift-waves of influence [initiation] that bring about the initial ripening of your mind-stream. On this very occasion you will attain the true meaning [of this path].

The second [actual foundational practice] has two sections:

(1) the way to establish a connection to the practical guide of the actual path, and

(2) a detailed explanation of the actual practice (101).

2.1.1 The Way to Establish a Connection to the Teaching on the Practical Guide of the Actual Path 101

In the *Nam kha' 'phrul mdzod* [*Treasury of Emanations from Space*] it says, "Three [types of] mistakes are described in Great Completion. The first pertains to mistakes that are repeated in Great Completion; Great Completion that makes mistakes regarding the pith instructions; and Great Completion that automatically cuts off mistakes [as they occur]." This practical guide pertains to the third [category of mistakes]. It is not the first one, where previous mistakes are repeated in Great Completion by putting the views of the eight [lower] vehicles into Great Completion in a way that contradicts the meaning of the equanimity of awakened awareness. However, when these [eight views] are not taken to be mistaken [through a higher Great Completion view], such mistakes are liberated into themselves.

In the *Ye khri mtha' sel* [*Removing the Extremes to the Primordial Throne*] it says, "The epitome of the Great Completion vehicle is [to realize] there is nothing to abandon, nor anything great to strive after. Don't strive for basis, path, and fruition [enlightenment]. You are liberated from grasping the [views of the] external and internal vehicles. It goes beyond abandoning or attaining some object of fruition. It is the basis of operation for those of best capacity."

[Second], Great Completion that makes mistakes in the pith instructions (102) is [for example] being bound by the wish for and attachment to greater and greater clarity, more and more emptiness, and [realizing] more and more just as it is. Therefore, these very [instructions] are not for the kind of person who wants an explanation in greater and greater detail. Set up [the mind] nakedly on the meaning of it [without attachment to] setting it up or having clarity. [In this way] mistakes and obscurations are automatically cut through.

This teaching is beyond the effort to accomplish anything in meditation. Its innate nature is that there is nothing to do. Its transparency does not change or transform in the three times. Because it never moves from its primordial purity, mistakes and disturbances [of mind] are left in their own way and are mixed with [awakened liveliness] so that mistakes are without reference point. For example, when a river coming from the mountains rises up [into a flood], the river's water carries and flings along all the plants and trees of the forest.

There are three kinds of practical guides: the way of practical guidance, the way of pointing out, and the way of a sojourner crossing over the mountains to an unfamiliar place. The ones given here are [the first] way of practical guidance. [The second] is giving the pointing out instructions of thoroughly cutting through and by-passing. [The third] pertains to the instructions for those lost in the foreign places of the after-death *bardos*. These [latter] two are subsumed under the first.

Those of lesser capacity (103) follow the practical guide gradually. What is to be realized, namely primordial wisdom's self-awakened awareness, gradually arises. What is to be purified, namely the stains of conceptual thought, gradually become purified. This profound skillful means to affect moving beyond *saṁsāra* I have already taught very extensively in the *sKu gsum rang shar* [*Self-Arising Three-fold Embodiment of Enlightenment*].

These instructions are given to those of sharpest capacity as total immersion in an instant, like lightning coming down. Through directly introducing primordial liberation in the [universal] basis and a path free of effort, and then having you make a decisive determination about these essential points, realization will come in its own place. The fruition will directly manifest itself in this very lifetime, and you will take your own seat regarding the primordial universal basis.

2.1.2 Detailed Explanation of the Actual Practice 103

The second, [the detailed explanation] has two divisions.

2.1.2.1 Different Capacities 103

Those of sharpest capacity don't have to meditate on anything. They cross over to liberation using the thoroughly cutting through instructions. Through their great diligence and the instructions on by-passing meditation, because of these, the three-fold embodiment of enlightenment is accomplished along the path of visions. Therefore, these are the instructions for liberation without any remaining aggregates [of the physical body].

First, there are two divisions based on differing capacities.

2.1.2.1.1 Lesser Capacity 103

First, here is the way it is pointed out for those of lesser capacity [as found in the] '*Bring po sor bzhag* [*Middling Teachings on Setting Up the Mind in its Own Place*]: "Pointing out appearances as mind (104). Pointing out mind as empty. Pointing out emptiness as clear-light. Pointing out the clear-light [of appearance/emptiness] as an inseparable pair. Pointing out the inseparable pair as great bliss." According to this passage, through pointing out appearances as mind, you reverse [the idea that appearances] are substantial and have their own characteristics. Through pointing out the mind as empty, you cut off conceptual thoughts in your own mind-stream that grasp appearances as real. Through pointing out emptiness as clear-light, you become liberated from getting lost in mistaken [views] about the nature of *dharmadhātu*. Through pointing out the clear-light as an inseparable pair, you have the inseparable pair of the expanse and [the liveliness of] awakened awareness [that arises in the expanse]. Through pointing out the inseparable pair as great bliss, you come to realize only the enlightened intention, namely the realization of the naked essence of emptiness/awakened awareness, free from the three—arising, staying, and ceasing.

Regarding this first system [of instructions for those of lesser capacity], I personally should give them the [proper] pith instructions. If you were to assert [what the pith instructions] might be like, they are like this: appearances do not seem to be mind because mind doesn't appear like this. If you were to ask, "Why would that be?" then this would be [due to] the appearance of [ripening] habitual karmic tendencies. Through the incidental conditions of the habitual karmic tendencies of the mind, [colorful] white and red appearances occur. Whatever appearances occur like this in their very essence do not inherently exist as real, but these appearances (105) are like a dream. Even appearances within a [night] dream, too, from the perspective of the mind being the dream, [appear] as if they are substantial, but in fact are insubstantial.

Likewise, if the appearances [caused by ripening] habitual karmic tendencies or by a deluded mind were to be taken as real, ultimately they are not experienced as inherently existing in the universal ground. There is no [difference between waking appearances and dreams], except for [the] interval [of time when they occur]. What appears [in the daytime] doesn't really appear, because it is without basis; and what appears in a [night] dream has the same manner of appearing [without basis].

Furthermore, the way to point out the mind series in Great Completion is as follows; *Bodhicitta* becomes the basis of arising of everything, like [waves in] the ocean. The liveliness of this is the basis of whatever appears, much like an aspect of the brightness of the ocean. What appears as the various play of this you should know to be like the arising of the planets and stars [on the surface of] the ocean. Regarding these three—[the basis, the liveliness, and the play]—from the perspective of the universal ground and *bodhicitta*, it is not possible to differentiate between them. That is because in the self-awakened mind these do not appear like that [as different]. For example, the three—the ocean itself, the aspect of the brightness [of the water], and the planets and stars that arise [as reflections] in it—cannot be identified as other than the essence of the water (106), but [only] seem [different]. From the perspective of the play [of appearances], when you analyze these here like this, there is no contradiction. With respect to the way these three appear—the ocean, the aspect of its brightness, and the [reflections of] the planets and stars—[they] only seem like [different] objects of the sense-organs. However, in that these appearances are without any real basis, both the appearance and the mind are mere designations without any basis. In the *Lus rgyud dang 'dra ba'i gdams pa* [*Instructions on the Similarity of the Body and Mind-Stream*] it says, "Do not engage in words about appearance and emptiness. Both are without any basis whatsoever." According to this passage, this [mind series teaching], also the way of *Mahamudrā*, is the skillful means only for guiding those of lesser capacity gradually along the path. The *Phyag khrid* [*Practical Guide*] by Bru rgyal ba, and those that followed him afterwards, have been quoted regarding their pith instructions. [Their teaching] is distinguished as a valid kind [of higher teaching], but it was not [generally] accepted. [Considering this] lower [level of teaching as comparable to] the enlightened intention of the higher Great Completion falls apart, just like [comparing] the sky to the earth.

2.1.2.1.2 Sharpest Capacity 106

Second, those of sharpest capacity [using the pith instruction series of teachings] should become liberated just from [hearing] the pointing out instructions. Therefore, it has two divisions:

(1) the actual pointing out, and

(2) crossing over with great non-action (107).

2.2 Actual Practice; Thoroughly Cutting Through 107

2.2.1 The Actual Pointing Out For Liberation 107

First, [the actual pointing out] has three divisions:

(1) commenting on the essential point,

(2) stopping and tying up, and

(3) binding.

2.2.1.1 Commenting on the Essential Point 107
First, has two divisions:

(1) pointing out the root, primordial awakened awareness, and

(2) pointing out the four—view, meditation, conduct, and fruition.

2.2.1.1.1 Pointing Out the Root, Primordial Awakened Awareness 107
The first has three divisions:

(1) all-encompassing awareness,

(2) reflection on awareness, and

(3) primordial awakened awareness.

2.2.1.1.1.1 All-Encompassing Awareness 107
First is the [awakened awareness] heart essence of a *Sugata*, whose aspiration simply encompasses all beings.

2.2.1.1.1.2 Reflection on Awareness 107
The second is from some vehicles where you meditate on awareness. If you don't meditate, you do not get this awareness. Even if you want to have it, it sometimes has clarity and sometimes is obscured.

2.2.1.1.1.3 Primordial Awakened Awareness 107
Third, is the primordial awakened awareness of Great Completion. This is the awakened awareness—whether you know it or not, or whether you meditate upon it or not. It is primordially arisen, primordially awakened. How is awakened awareness known? Externally, appearances are insubstantial. Internally, the mind is selfless and awakens by itself. In between, conceptual thought arises together, vanishes together, and is

primordially aware together.

Pointing out the truth of this is as follows: The student assumes the seven-fold essential body points, and establishes [the mind] directly on awakened awareness without mental construction and unadulterated (108). The lama says [to the student], "Ah, fortunate child of the lineage! Look nakedly to see in yourself if there is any agent of your reflecting or your being aware. Is there a duality between an agent of looking and an object looked at? Through turning inward and reversing the [dualistic] mind as non-dual, they occur by their own nature, openly, like space.

In that, do not do anything to change even a hair of this, because the real nature of this is inexpressible; inseparable pairs of the clarity/emptiness and mind/appearance can never be impeded by any name whatsoever. You cannot know this by determining this by example, by expression, or by conceptually analyzing it. What is transparent cannot be abandoned. It is free of skillful means, without basis, rootless. It is all-pervasive emptiness. Its clarity is unobstructed. It is more and more awake. Its primordial liberation becomes more and more transparent. Its self-occurring brightness becomes clearer and clearer. Its bliss without an antidote becomes more and more vibrant. As primordially arisen, it is bare and more and more naked. Awakened awareness never knows distraction. Its clear-light is without seeing. Its natural disposition is uninterrupted. Its nature can't be expressed in words. Its primordial wisdom can never be abandoned (109). Its lucid appearance is selfless. The sparkling immediacy of the mind is non-conceptual. Its primordial wisdom does not separate subject and object. This wakeful empty space and openness of mind without essence is the secret path of Great Completion. This is the heart-blood of mothers and *ḍākinī*s. This is the inheritance of Dran pa Nam mkha'. This is the special instruction of *Rig pa Rang shar*. How wonderful that someone understands or realizes this! *E ma ho*! If we were to elaborate on this through the scriptures, in the *Kun bzang thugs kyi brnag pa* [*Reflections of the Heart-Mind of Kun tu bZang Po*], it says, "How wonderful is this precious swastika! How incorruptible is this house of the life-force! How wonderful is it that it is stable and unchanging! How wonderful is its all-pervasive clarity! How wonderful is its unborn spontaneous presence! How wonderful is its primordial purity! Because it is self-arisen it is unmistaken. By encountering the expanse, it can't be reversed. Through realizing its ultimate truth, there is its enlightened bliss body, which is pure white and shining. Out of limitless sentient beings, none have found it. By dismantling the physical aggregates, it is self-appearing. It stays as sacred *bodhicitta*. In being pervaded by immense *bodhicitta* (110), then self-arising primordial wisdom arises clearly. Free of birth and death, it is pure inspiration. Without ever separating from or uniting to it, it is pure inspiration." Also, in the *Ye khri mtha' sel* [*Removing the Extremes to the Primordial Throne*] it says, "The eternal mind is unchanging. The eternal mind is unelaborated. The eternal mind is without birth and death. The eternal mind is without ever separating from it or uniting to it. The eternal mind is impartial and non-sectarian. The eternal mind is non-conceptual. The eternal mind is free of making something happen or stopping anything. The eternal mind is free of being more or less. The eternal mind is effortless." Also, in the *Mu med brdal pa's rgyud* [*Tantra of Limitless Pervasion*], it says, "In essence, there is nothing like this. There is no root to the occurrence and dissolving of everything. How could it have a top if it has no roots? For that reason how can higher and lower regions exist? Transparent awakened awareness has arisen in the expanse. There is no clarity, nor is there darkness day or night. Everything is balanced and stays evenly. It has no particular place or other place. It is completed as the one great sphere without construction." Also, in the *Seng ge sgrags* [*Lion's Roar*] it says, "Everything, everywhere is without inside or outside. Its primordial original purity is never abandoned and cannot be known through mental construction (111). Its innate nature is primordial enlightenment. This one great sphere is the *dharmakāya*, which is free from definable characteristics, like space. This is the best view much like a roaring lion." So it is said.

2.2.1.1.2 Pointing Out the Four—View, Meditation, Conduct, Fruition 111

2.2.1.1.2.1 View 111

Second, there are four ways to be free from view and the practice of meditation. The first is that this kind of awakened awareness is such that it is the actual foundational practice of everything in *saṁsāra* and *nirvāṇa*, including appearances as substantial, insubstantial, both, and as non-dual, such that nothing whatsoever is abandoned. Even though appearances seem to be substantial, in fact they are just like the play of dreams and illusions. Because no essence inherently exists, they never go beyond being insubstantial. Because nothing appears as substantial or insubstantial, these two names are mere designations and names without basis. Because they are free from being accepted as either existing or not-existing, they are not known as going beyond the unelaborated *dharmadhātu*. Even when looking especially into this, there is no existing duality, nor agent in the *dharmadhātu*. Without any inherent nature, this goes beyond anything viewed or an agent of viewing. Even when not viewing, it doesn't go anywhere else, and no basis can be found (112). This is called "the view of the domain of space of the great primordial liberation." From the ninth chapter of the *Nam mkha' dbyings yangs rgyud* [*Tantra of the Vast Expanse of Space*] it says, "That which arises as the actual foundation of everything is the realization of awakened awareness, the awakened mind-itself, completely purified, primordially free of [all] causes and conditions, free of color and shape, and beyond exaggeration and denigration. Everything that arises does not stay. There is nothing to abandon in the one [great] interconnected [sphere] because everything abandoned co-emerges, arising as the actual foundation and its completion. This is the great basis of all existing phenomena. For that reason everything done serves *bodhicitta*. Nothing inherently existing, yet it arises as the basis of everything."

Well, if you were to ask if you will get these instructions, the answer is you will. Because of not searching for setting up the view, it will become liberated into its own nature. Through not having to grasp to understand this, you will be liberated from [the need for] any remedy. Through not having any cause to [engage in] meditation practice, you will be liberated from [the need for] meditating. There will be liberation from [the need to] purify any grasping, such as ordinary appearance, attachments to certain vehicles, attachment to the play of meditative experiences, and being bound by expectation [of gain] or fear [of not getting it].

2.2.1.1.2.2 Meditation 112

Second, with respect to meditating on that, you will not find an agent of meditation (113), nor will you find an object [that] is meditated on. Meditation is transparent knowing, which does not grasp with conceptual thought, which has wide-open clarity and is carefree. This very [kind of meditation] is called "self-arisen meditation that transcends conceptual thought." Even when not meditating, there is no essence, so it is never lost; so it is incorrect to do anything. Because it doesn't have a particular name in the three times, it is called "the great self-liberation in the domain of space." In the *Ye khri mtha' sel* [*Removing Extremes to the Primordial Throne*] it says, "It pervades everywhere in the *dharmadhātu* without falling into any partiality. The awakened mind-itself stays without waxing and waning. Meditation practice arises in the immense vastness. All sorts of meditations are the great self-clarity." Well, if you were to ask, at this time do you accept or reject appearance, the answer is that appearance is like the appearance of a dream. Even when [such appearances] are unobstructed and vivid, if you appreciate the essential point about the ordinary deluded mind becoming purified in the *dharmadhātu*, then you will no longer conceptualize about [appearing] objects.

When you wake up from sleep, the appearance of dreams is self-purified; likewise, for one who has attained enlightenment then all deluded appearances self-disappear. Therefore, you should not engage in acceptance or rejection of anything (114). From the *Mu med brdal ba'i rgyud* [*Tantra of Limitless Pervasiveness*], it says, "One who sees appearances as existing is mistaken by grasping them as permanent and viewing them as substantial. One who sees appearances as non-existing is mistaken by view of nihilism or nothingness." Furthermore, in the *Seng ge sgra ba sgrags* [*Lion's Roar*] it says, "Set up [the view] free from distinguishing between appearance and non-appearance." Well, if you were to ask at that time, what if conceptual thought doesn't arise about the object, the answer is that primordial wisdom arises by itself, from the very moment [directly] knowing the object arises, and it arises without any basis and without any agent. Everything dissolves into primordial wisdom, which is self-occurring in its own place, much like the sun and its rays. In fact, the essence and liveliness of primordial wisdom is self-occurring and non-dual, without either gathering or emanating. Free of all elaboration, it remains as the state of *dharmakāya*.

Some people say that conceptual thought is self-occurring primordial wisdom and is the *dharmakāya*, but this doesn't discriminate or make a distinction between essence and liveliness. This ordinary mind, wherein objects arise, [and the mind that] follows after the object as existing or not-existing, however, is not self-occurring primordial wisdom. At the time it has arisen, it has no inherent existence, (115) and so it arises as primordial wisdom's liveliness. With respect to not having the realization, conceptual thought goes its own way and becomes the cause of continuing in *saṁsāra*. Thus, with respect to this vehicle, because awakened awareness pervades everything, whatever moves is its liveliness. At the very place where it arises, there is no arising, and it becomes self-purified. Therefore, some others recognize it as the view that sets [whatever arises] free. When meditation is joined to conceptual thought, however beneficial, it is none other than the seeds of *saṁsāra*. Therefore, without viewing and without analyzing with conceptual thought, it disappears by itself, without a fixation point.

There are three ways to become liberated from conceptual thought. Liberation from the benefit or harm of conceptual thought has the conventional [metaphor] of being like a thief in an empty house, because what you seek to find is lost or was never there. In fact, regarding whatever seems to stay or move, if the agent that recognizes itself is not free from being baseless and free from extremes, you will not reach the enlightened intention of this supreme vehicle. At that time, if there is no elaboration of conceptual thought toward the object, if it stays in its own place, in a relaxed state, then this is called the "meditative experience of non-conceptual stillness" (116). At that time, the aspect of awakened awareness that is lucid and bright is known as the "*dharmakāya*." Again, remaining more and more open in emptiness is the experience of emptiness. At that time, the aspect of awakened awareness that is vivid and awake is known as "*dharmakāya*."

Furthermore, the joy fades more and more. The bliss remains and as it becomes more and more vibrant, it is called "the meditative experience of bliss." At that time, the aspect of awakened awareness that is pristine and open is "*dharmakāya.*"

Furthermore, the pristine clarity remains and becomes what is called "the meditative experience of luminosity." At that time, the aspect of awakened awareness that is transparent is called "*dharmakāya.*"

Therefore, at any point in time, awakened awareness emerges as without basis, naked, and as clear wakefulness. Cultivating this is the bottom line of this supreme vehicle meditation practice. It is the quintessence of views. It is the heart stone of meditation.

2.2.1.1.2.3 **Conduct** 116

Third, at the time of the four kinds of [bodily] activities, when external appearances appear, since they are without inherent nature, you won't grasp after conceptual thought [about perceptions] as real. At the time that internal conceptual thoughts arise, since they are without essence you won't even be close to becoming attached to them. In this natural primordial liberation of appearance/mind, you won't generate any waves of delusion. In that awakened awareness is transparent (117) and bare and is no longer covered by conceptual thought, you will establish it as an infinite vast expanse. The three gateways [remain] alertly relaxed. Appearances are carefree. Conduct is naturally unfolding. Conduct is free of fear and doubt. Such conduct in any given situation is free of making something happen or stopping something from happening, and is free of accepting and rejecting. Doing whatever [best fits the situation] is called "mastery of conduct that is the great naked liberation." In the *Ye khri mtha' sel nam mkha' dkar po'i rgyud* [*Tantra of Pure Space that Removes Extremes to the Primordial Throne*] it says, "Do not obstruct anything that is arising by itself. If you do not engage the conduct, how is it obstructed? Such conduct is self-conduct that is primordially uninhibited. By conducting yourself that way, where is the progress in practice? Practitioners carry unobstructedness in its own way. This is the great mastery of conduct." Well, if you were to ask, if you let deluded appearances be and let go of them, won't they become something ordinary, the answer is that which is ordinary becomes deluded through self-grasping. Because awakened awareness has arisen in such *yogis*, they know that whatever arises is without basis, and all delusion is cleared up through [the realization of] awakened awareness. Previously, it has been said, "The definition of self-arisen awakened awareness is that because it is non-dual, it clears away dualistic appearance (118). Because it is self-occurring, it clears away causes and conditions. Because it is spontaneously present, it clears away expectation [of gain and] of fear [of not getting it]. Because it purifies, it clears away stains. Because it is clear, it clears away nihilism. Because it is without substance, it clears away eternalism." Also, in the *gSer gyi rus sbal* [*Golden Tortoise*] it says, "When the genuine truth of awakened awareness has arisen, everything becomes clear in its very essence, free of obscurations."

2.2.1.1.2.4 **Fruition** 118

Fourth, the fruition is also spontaneously present in the view, meditation, and conduct. For example, wherever a person goes he can't go beyond this earth; likewise, even if he takes the view and does the meditation, he never goes beyond fruition's own place. Therefore, through there being nothing to be purified and nothing to flourish, the practitione is free of hope [of gain]. Because there is no place to fall into *saṁsāra*, they cut off the continuation of the fear [of not getting it]. As all phenomena of *saṁsāra* and *nirvāṇa*, as primordially pure and primordially clear, arise as self-occurring primordial wisdom, therefore, this primordial crossing over to the fruition is called "the great ultimate liberation, the mastery of fruition." In the *Seng ge sgra ba sgrags* [*Lion's Roar*] it says, "Everything is subsumed under and saturated by energy drops—everything without exception (119). This is the bliss of mastery. What has been called 'suffering' has no name. Everything without exception is primordial *Buddhahood*." Well, if you were to think about how certain types of sentient beings become directly deluded, they become deluded from not having a realization like this. In the *Gab pa dgu bskor* [*Cycle of the Nine Hidden Secrets*] it says, "Now, there is a big difference between having and not having the realization. They are obscured by not having the realization. The essence of the five causes [of rebirth] is the wrong way."

2.2.1.2 **Stopping and Tying Up**[6] 119

Second, the key to the view is tying up [the view of] everything [as empty in the moment] like lightning flashing. For that reason, there is no construction whatsoever about mind and appearance, so that it arises vividly in its own way. It is viewed in the *dharmadhātu* vividly [and instantly] without delusion, much like seeing lightning flashing. In the *Nam mkha' 'phrul gyi mdzod chen* [*Great Treasury of Magical Display from Space*] it says, "At the very moment they arise, appearances and mind are viewed as vivid, clear, and bright. Because they are self-arising, free of causes and conditions, they are like lightning flashing. Because they are without switching or transforming and self-arising, they are like lightning flashing. Because they are free of making something happen or stopping something from happening, they are like lightning flashing. Because they are self-arising through the great self-occurrence, they are (120) like lightning flashing." According to this passage, the key to everything about meditation is tied to immediately occurring awakened awareness. For that reason, at the very moment conceptual thought arises, it is liberated into self-occurring awakened awareness. This is instantaneous meditation.

As was previously said, "It is called 'instantaneous' because conceptual thought has no place where it is born. It is 'instantaneous' because whatever has arisen is self-arisen, therefore not recognizing [awakened awareness] has no place to hide. It is called 'instantaneous' because awakened awareness and appearance are like stone meeting bone. It is called 'instantaneous' because those [two] are without any mental construction. It is called 'instantaneous' because besides this there is nothing to meditate on." According to this passage, the key to all conduct is tying it to automatically occurring primordial wisdom. For that reason, any conduct pertaining to the four [bodily] activities is unconstructed, and when such conduct goes its own way, this is automatic primordial wisdom.

Previously it was said, "Nothing in particular is stopped, so it comes by its own force [automatically]. Nothing in particular is done, so it comes by its own force [automatically]. By not contradicting anything done, it

---

6. *'gag bsdam pa*: "stopping and tying up."

comes by its own force [automatically]. By whatever conduct arising as the play of the *dharmadhātu*, it comes by its own force [automatically]. Because there is neither the three—letting go of, gathering, or wanting— it comes by its own force [automatically]. In bringing everything (121) into the domain of space of *dharmadhātu*, wherein nothing either agrees with or disagrees with this, it comes by its own force [automatically]. Because the three gateways (body, speech, and mind] remain carefree in every way, in every [situation], and there is no need of any antidote, they remain open, carefree, and empty. The mind is happy." According to this passage, the key to all fruition is tied up with the springing forth[7] of the three-fold enlightened bodies in the domain of space. For that reason, whatever arises and whatever appears is finished with judgments or biases, and becomes the fruition by which the three-fold embodiment of enlightenment springs forth in the domain of space.

Previously it was said, "The springing forth of *dharmakāya* is space. The springing forth of *sambhogakāya* is [the elements] earth, water, fire, and wind. The springing forth of *nirmāṇakāyas* is the six realms of sentient beings. The springing forth of primordial wisdom is the five poisons. The springing forth of awakened awareness is wherein nothing is abandoned and everything is taken as path." Well, if you were to ask, how can *saṁsāra* that needs to be purified ever come to an end, there is no contradiction. It is not like that because for Great Completion *yogis* primordial awakened awareness will arise, and it appears like this. In the *Me long dgu 'dus 'od gsal gyi rgyud* [*Tantra of the Clear-Light of the Collection of the Nine Mirrors*] it says (122), "The meaning of the view is like a thunderbolt falling from the sky without resistance. The meaning of meditation is like the sun arising in the sky, so that all the darkness disappears, or like lightning falling. The meaning of conduct is like a flood gushing forth in some area washing away the plants, trees, earth, and rocks. The meaning of the fruition is like finding a precious wish-granting jewel that brings together and accomplishes whatever you need or desire."

---

7. *klong brdol*: "springing forth."

2.2.1.3 Binding[8] 122

Third, binding. You have to make a determination about view, meditation, conduct, and fruition pertaining [specifically] to [or bound to moment-by-moment] present appearances, which are without basis, yet are unceasing.

In summary, awakened awareness of the *dharmadhātu* is subsumed under the one great interconnected sphere.

(1) Binding is beyond obstruction.

(2) It is effortless.

(3) It goes beyond all limits.

(4) The essential point is that *saṁsāra* and *nirvāṇa* become liberated without division.

(5) This is crossing over to the *dharmadhātu* free of birth and cessation. This is binding with the five essential points.

2.2.2 The Great Non-Action for Crossing Over 122

Second, the great non-action for crossing over has three divisions:

(1) explaining the general meaning of removing faults (123),

(2) explaining the nature of non-action in particular, and

(3) explaining the confidence in meditative practice.

2.2.2.1 Explaining the General Meaning of Removing Faults 123

First, well, if you were to ask, isn't everything in *saṁsāra* and *nirvāṇa* liberated, whether realized or not realized, continuously in its characteristics across the three times, without any before or after and without beginning and end, it would follow that there is a flaw [in this thinking] wherein [you think] that there is no need to do anything. The answer is that there are twelve phenomena relevant to not doing, and through these you cross over to the supreme effortless not doing. From doing too much, you wander in *saṁsāra*. In the *sPros bral nam mkha' dang mnyam*

---

8. *chings su bcing ba*: "binding."

pa'i rgyud [*Tantra Equal to Unelaborated Space*] it says, "If there is any more doing [than this], you will not stay in the genuine truth. If you make too much effort, you will go astray as the best disciple of [the] demoness Mara. Set up the mind relaxed and loose, undistracted from the truth, self-liberating [all] doing." According to this passage, isn't this a contradiction in wanting to attain something [by not doing]? [The answer is that such] contradictions are brought into the path. Appearances are brought [into the path] as friends. This is called "whatever is done becomes the practice [of emptiness of doing]."

2.2.2.2 Explaining the Nature of Not Doing in Particular 123

Second, there are three divisions, which are: four aims, three capacities of confidence, and five phenomena for crossing over via not doing (124).

2.2.2.2.1 The Four Aims 124

First, one must have the four aims[9] [which are]:

(1) being able to do the opposite of what is [typically] done to accomplish,

(2) not being afraid of others' criticism,

(3) the mind not engaging in characteristic activities, and

(4) not chasing after fame and conventions.

2.2.2.2.2 The Three Capacities of Confidence[10] 124

Second,

(1) [when you have] occasional supernormal abilities, or there are certainly many subtle signs of progress, even if you were to see the serene light of Kun tu bZang po, you would have made a determination that this is none other than your own mind. [As a result] you don't generate any elation [about such experiences] and don't go astray [getting attached to them]; this is the full measure of confidence.

---

9. *dgos pa bzhi*: "four aims."
10. *gding tshad*: "capacities of confidence."

(2) There [still] will certainly be many occasional conditions that support sickness and suffering. Yet, even if the King of the Hell Realms were to pour molten hot metal into your mouth, and you saw yourself being burned by flesh-eating demons, you will have made a determination that these are none other than self-appearing [visions of your own mind]. Since you no longer fall into fear or despair, this is the full measure of confidence.

(3) There are certainly many ways to become famous for Bon teachings and logic. If you have directly heard the eternal *Sugatas, bodhisattvas*, or sTon pa g.Shen rab explaining the Bon teachings under his own umbrella (125), you will have made the determination that these are just your own self-appearing visions [of your own mind]. Since you no longer [blindly] chase after their words [because of the extent of your realizations], this is the full measure of confidence of the Great Completion tenets, and you never turn back from that.

Thus, you will have cut off relying on fear or hope regarding the phenomena of *saṁsāra* and *nirvāṇa*, respectively. If you don't have fear and despair, it is no longer necessary to do any practice. If you still do not have the full measure of confidence in these ways, [you will fall into] a bad abyss. When you have been seized by doubt, you fall back again [into *saṁsāra*].

2.2.2.2.3 The Five Phenomena for Crossing-Over via Not Doing 125

Third, this has five divisions:

2.2.2.2.3.1 No Buddhahood by the Phenomena of Doing 125

First, there is no *Buddhahood* through the activity of doing. All doing is [based on] the formative [aggregate]. Therefore, all formative aggregates are impermanent. The meaning of not-doing is like space. [With respect to space], nothing is accomplished by doing or by effort, and because of that you cross over to the great freedom from doing and beyond effort. As was previously said, "One who stays in the meaning free of doing, beyond effort, with nothing to accomplish, and who has taken up a body of one of the six classes of sentient beings—whether god or human—his awakened mind-itself is primordially pure in the domain of space of genuine *dharmadhātu*. Whoever aspires for guidance on this path should not use any effort, and should stay on the meaning of this."

2.2.2.2.3.2 Without Relying on any Remedy 126

Second (126), because you are without any tendency whatsoever that is not in accordance with what is to be abandoned, there is no need to rely on any remedy in your mind-stream. Everything is purified and you cross over to the great blissful *Buddha* realms of clear-light. In the *Kun bzang bde ba'i lung* [*The Prophesies of Blissful Kun tu bZang po*] it says, "The *maṇḍala* of the Victorious Ones is the golden seat. Everything outside and inside is subsumed together. This [all] is none other than the great bliss itself. This is never moving from *Buddhahood*."

2.2.2.2.3.3 Whatever Arises is the Play of Primordial Wisdom 126

Third, whatever arises like this arises again and again as the play of self-occurring primordial wisdom. Because these are the ornaments of *dharmadhātu*, which arise in-and-by-themselves, this is where primordial wisdom springs forth, and everything crosses over into the expanse of one taste and evenness. In the *bDe gshegs dgongs pa 'dus pa'i rgyud* [*Tantra of Gathering the Enlightened Intentions of the Sugatas*] it says, "The winds of conceptual thought become activated and move, but the expanse of self-occurring primordial wisdom never degenerates. [Everything] is subsumed under and consummated in the great spontaneous presence. This is the great fruition of complete purity thorough liberation. This is the clear-light of stainless primordial wisdom. The [great] multiplicity of appearances are the ornaments of this play [of the liveliness of awakened awareness]."

2.2.2.2.3.4 All Phenomena Arise From the Expanse of *Dharmadhātu* 126

Fourth, all phenomena of *saṁsāra* and *nirvāṇa* that occur arise from the expanse of the *dharmadhātu* (127). Everything becomes liberated just as it arises. Therefore, you cross over to great primordial liberation and you don't need to determine that it is liberated again. As it says in the tenth chapter [of the *bDe gshegs dgongs pa 'dus pa'i rgyud* [*Tantra of Gathering the Enlightened Intentions of the Sugatas*], "Make a decisive determination about any mistakes and obscurations. Primordially it exists beyond the words of eternalism and nihilism. What is primordially liberated is not accomplished and unobstructed. This is the complete purification of the great self-liberation."

2.2.2.2.3.5 **Liberation From Extremes** 127

Fifth, through having realized self-occurring awakened awareness, it doesn't get better, and you are liberated from the extreme of *nirvāṇa*. Through not having realized this, it doesn't get worse, and you are liberated from the extreme of *saṁsāra*. By this view, you cut off the tendency to partial views and partial realizations. You won't become sectarian, and therefore you are liberated from the extremes of the eight vehicles. Whatever is done is already primordially liberated. There is nothing to view, nothing to meditate on, and nothing to accomplish. Through being without doing and without effort, you will remain in a happy carefree state of mind, and this will suffice.

2.2.2.3 **Explaining the Confidence of Meditative Practice** 127

Third, explaining the confidence of meditative practice is as follows: Well, if you were to ask, if there is non-doing toward all phenomena, then is there no purpose to all the views and conduct of the eight stages [vehicles], the answer is that these all have effort and can't accomplish (128) effortlessness. Therefore, even if you don't engage with it, you will automatically attain the positive qualities of these, and by knowing all this as the self-play [of lively awakened awareness], through that you will eradicate all mistakes. As was said in the previous [cited text],

"For example, when a very powerful horse runs, the plants [under its hooves] are automatically ruined. Likewise, all these vehicles that are endowed with effort, through the great influence of the king of awakened awareness automatically it [the effort] falls down at its very roots. Without effort, this is the self-occurring fruition. This completes the enlightened intention [within your own mind-stream] without [the need for] progress. From the beginning, without grasping, this is spontaneously accomplished." By this passage, the real nature is Great Completion without doing anything whatsoever. When you are resting day and night without doing anything, and are without fear, this is the view. If you spend months and years on this, this is the meditation. What is always self-occurring without obstruction, this is the conduct. Letting awakened awareness go wherever it wants, this is the meditative experience of enlightened intention. Not viewing conceptual thought as an enemy, this is the skillful means of fixing the mind. [According to these] special instructions, do not restrict, do not try to change the five poisons. Neither accepting nor rejecting virtue and vice, this is the *yogic* discipline (129). Not secretly rejecting what is not in accordance with this, this is the fruition. Not relying on [using an] antidote in your mind-stream, this is the spiritual duty. Automatically letting go of all actions done and to be done, this is enlightened activity. The place of liberation is left in its own way; therefore, it is the path beyond expectation of gain or fear of not getting it. Whether you do or do not realize this, everything is self-liberated. This is the full measure of understanding and realization. All phenomena become the one [state] of non-doing.

Well, if you were to ask doesn't this state [of not doing] tend toward one side, nihilism, the answer is that understanding the truth comes through not doing. As for doing anything, it is unobstructed [without mental engagement]. As for doing anything, there is no attachment to it. As for not doing anything, it is unobstructed. As for not doing anything, there is no attachment. This unobstructedness is self-arising. This non-attachment is self-liberating. Because whatever activity is done never passes beyond the domain of space of self-arising/self-liberated, you never fall into going astray.

2.3 **Attaining the Truth—By-Passing** 129

The second part explaining the by-passing path of liberation through meditation has two divisions:

(1) why by-passing is the higher way, and

(2) explaining the actual teachings of this special path.

2.3.1 Why By-Passing is the Higher Way 129

First, in the *Ye khri* [*Removing Extremes to the Primordial Throne*] it says, "There are ten ways to explain how [by-passing] is exalted [over thoroughly cutting through]. This explanation will be summarized in seven points (130).

2.3.1.1 Purifying Dualistic Grasping 130

First, is the difference of purifying dualistic grasping. In thoroughly cutting through, [material] objects like mountains, rocks, and so forth are without basis, so that this grasping mind will simply not affect sealing [everything] as self-liberated. Having [residual] substantiality, you will not be able to make it [completely] self-purified. By-passing [practice] relies upon the visions of the five lights in the expanse, and through the purification of external objects as being light, there will be direct liberation from all dualistic grasping. In the *Ye khri* [*Removing Extremes to the Primordial Throne*] it says, "All dualistic grasping doesn't stay and becomes completely purified. In this state there is complete enlightenment."

2.3.1.2 The Distinction of the Self-Appearance of the Aggregates of the Physical Body 130

Second, is the difference regarding the self-appearing aggregates of the physical body. When purifying it in thoroughly cutting through practice, the subtlest particles of the physical body do not become light. They don't change into light, yet there is some change into the illusory body, and not all the sense-fields are cut off in the end. If you do not attain the body of light, these practices will not [help you] attain divine eyes, supernormal abilities, the identity of the great waves of the magical display, or the enlightened great consciousness-transference [rainbow body]. From relying on [this residual physical body], you will never be able to extensively serve the welfare of sentient beings. In by-passing practice, the form aggregate of the physical body [completely] becomes self-appearing light-itself. The other aggregates are also [completely] purified in their own way. Through accomplishing this enlightened immortal body, you will serve the purpose of all sentient beings until they are emptied from *saṁsāra* (131). In the previous text it says, "The five aggregates are not abandoned but are purified as visions. It is great because it is purified as self-appearance."

2.3.1.3 The Distinction of Purifying Consciousness 131

Third, is the difference of purifying the sense-consciousnesses. In thoroughly cutting through practice, deluded appearances are not obstructed. By relying on subjective and objective phenomena, and not obstructing the deluded mind, it is difficult to bring liberation quickly. In by-passing practice, by purifying the objects of consciousness, [delusion] is automatically reversed. Through being without any view as subject and object, deluded visions remain nameless. Object and mind are self purified, and become liberated into [pure realm] male and female *bodhisattvas*. From this [same text] it says, "There are eight objects of the eight consciousnesses, self-appearing as the eight female *bodhisattvas*. They are spontaneously present in a state absent of searching. This is the great signature of self-appearing primordial wisdom."

2.3.1.4 Serving the Purpose of Others by Directly Seeing the Clear-Light [From the Viewpoint that] Nothing Inherently Exists 131

Fourth, through directly seeing the clear-light, you can't serve the purpose of sentient beings other than yourself. Awakened awareness exists primordially as a body of light. In thoroughly cutting through practice, it is said that, through the encounter with emptiness, you will not see the light in yourself. There is no liberation of appearing objects as (132) self-appearing clear-light. Because the view is not abandoned toward others, you serve the purpose of these beings by doing for others. In by-passing practice, by penetrating the essential point, when the essence of awakened awareness is taken internally, at that time, this radiant light of awakened awareness that sees beyond becomes clear outside, and everything is liberated as self-appearing clear-light. Therefore, there is no need to act to serve the purpose of sentient beings other than you. In this [same text] it says, "It occurs from itself and appears to itself. Through this radiant state you become free of [all] objects. This great self-appearance is without objects. It is greater because the other doesn't have this kind of welfare toward sentient beings. Well, you might ask that if sentient beings are known as self-appearances, then will it not happen that you won't serve the purposes of sentient beings? The answer is that even if you know this as self-appearing, you also [still] serve the purpose of sentient beings.

2.3.1.5 The Distinction of Not Searching for the Fruition 132

Fifth, is the difference of not searching for the fruition. In thoroughly cutting through practice, having subdued appearances and cut through the coarse appearances, the [full] fruition will be hidden. In by-passing practice, because the visions reach full measure, the fruition comes directly, and because of that there is no need to set it up. Attaining the [full] fruition directly in this very lifetime is described in the [same text] as previously, where it says, "This is the fruition free of searching. It is greater because without searching for it, it is [already] spontaneously present" (133).

2.3.1.6 The Distinction of Directly Seeing the Self-Visions 133

Sixth, is the difference of directly seeing the self-visions. In thoroughly cutting through practice, the gateways of the six senses are not [completely] purified. You need to search for the brightness of mind. In by-passing practice, by opening the gateways of clear-light by the winds of primordial wisdom, the visions of the four lamps appear, and through that all deluded appearances become [completely] self-purified. Having realized these all as self-appearing, you encounter [these visions] as the radiant light rays of the *dharmadhātu*, and, as a result, you remain without [either] uniting with or separating from ultimate truth. In this [same text] it says, "Through realizing the true meaning of [the visions being] self-appearing, this is greater because in truth you are never united with or separated from it."

2.3.1.7 The Distinction of the Levels [of Development] 133

Seventh, is the difference of the levels [of development]. In thoroughly cutting through practice, you are not able to reach the full measure of both the visions and the body, but just in the mind. [In by-passing] you are brought into the fact of non-engagement. You reach the unchanging, eternal, immense ground. As previously it was said, "This unchanging, eternal ground is the great way because ultimately it is the non-engagement [of everything appearing]."

2.3.2 Explaining the Actual Teaching for the Secret Path; The Essential Point of the Pith Instructions to Establish Certainty 133

[The Methods from the *Awakened Awareness of the Cuckoo*]

Second, the essential point of the pith instructions to establish certainty is found in four sections of the *Rig pa khu byug* [*Awakened Awareness of the Cuckoo*] where it says:

> The king of self-knowing awakened awareness (134) is *bodhicitta* itself. To serve the welfare of sentient beings it manifests magically as a body, which is called "the powerful bird with the extra-long beak." This bird comes out from a nest that looks like red rocks with white streaks. His lung passages are like the four [major] mothers, and four [minor] sons. Four [princes] riding on horses act to serve the welfare of sentient beings at all times. These horses, which are emanations of thoroughbreds, when they move and travel, the four great kings lift up each horse by its four legs. The four queens of the [respective] four seasons support him at the [four] sides. The four emanating winds lift him and move him. The four great rivers are the continuous flow of his merit. The four emanating fires balance the temperature. [All] have their place in the golden earth. Eight clear mirrors adorn their enlightened bodies. Three secret seed syllables manifest as their enlightened heart-minds. The five radiant lamps are generated from the crown of his head. All the stars and planets shine from his waist. The four attendants serve him (135). He unceasingly serves the benefit of sentient beings and does this all the time. These are the positive qualities that come from the horses.

According to this passage, [it contains all] the essential points of the clear-light by-passing practices. These were taught by Kun tu bZang po to the *ḍākinīs*, who were bound to encrypt them. Many earlier supreme scholars appeared but did not decode them until I found the opportunity to understand a portion of this.

The bird with the extra-long beak pertains to the radiance of awakened awareness [manifesting] as the light rays [of the visions]. Therefore, this long-beaked bird is said [to symbolize] the radiance of awakened awareness. Awakened awareness stays in the center of your heart. From the heart comes a single channel about the size of a wheat straw where it connects to the lungs. The interior of this channel is filled with winds. By means of these winds, the radiance of awakened awareness is activated, and also from their agitation all conceptual thought occurs. That is called "ordinary mind." The wind is like a blind horse having legs, and the mind is like a lame person having eyes mounted [on the horse]. When the winds become calm, the radiance dissolves into awakened awareness, and the fluctuation of conceptual thought has become purified. The basis of arising of clear-light is established as having the three characteristics—essence, nature, and compassion—and these are unobstructed (136). By penetrating the profound essential points of by-passing, having activated the radiance of primordial wisdom through the winds, and having purified the channel of light, this brings the full measure of [the visions] arising at the gateways of the far reaching lasso [of the eye lamps]. Having purified the [impure visions in the] gateways of *saṁsāra*, you enjoy the [pure] visions of primordial wisdom. For that reason, forty-two profound essential points of by-passing have been taught, and these are described according to stages.

2.3.2.1 Four Great Kings 136

When the text says, "the four great kings lift up the horse by its four legs," this pertains to four essential points:

(1) the essential points of body, speech, and mind;

(2) the essential point of the [eye] gateways that make the visions;

(3) the essential point of the basis of arising of the object [the visions]; and

(4) the essential point of slowing the winds and awakened awareness's [liveliness]. When the prince of the Mu king[11] went to the four great kings to elevate the king, at that time he ruled the three realms. Similarly, by being elevated by these four types of essential points, [the king of] awakened awareness gains control over the [pure] visions of primordial wisdom.

2.3.2.1.1 The Essential Points of Body, Speech, and Mind 136

The first of these has three divisions.

2.3.2.1.1.1 Body 136

First, is having suitable support of the body to make the channels and winds serviceable (137). Through that [holding the body points], the clear-light directly arises, and because of that, it is very important to penetrate the essential point of the body. In the *gSer gyi phreng ba mdzes pa* [*The Beautiful Golden Rosary*] it says, "The *dharmakāya* posture is like a lion sitting. The *sambhogakāya* posture is like an elephant sitting. The *nirmāṇakāya* posture is like a *rishi* sitting." According to this passage, it is taught that being endowed with each of these respective postures has two purposes.

Dharmakāya posture 137

First, the *dharmakāya* posture is like a lion sitting. Squat in a crouching posture with [the balls of] both feet [on the ground] and the shins of the legs placed toward the ground. Straighten the back and restrain the lower gate a little. Put the weight of the head on the neck. The fingers of both hands in a fist are planted [on the ground] in between both legs. Some say that the soles of the feet are placed [fully] on the ground, but in our tradition this practice is a little different, according to those who have previously taught it. The purpose [of the posture] is that by enough wind made to move, the central channel opens. [Because of that] the external visions will immediately arise. Internally, the enlightened intention of the *dharmakāya* arises free of all conceptual thought.

---

11. The Mu king is the father of sTon pa g.Shen rab, who is the prince.

Sambhogakāya posture 137

Second, the *sambhogakāya* posture is like an elephant (138) lying down. Squat [and kneel forward] with both [feet] on the ground, with the knees joined to the chest [and the elbows on the ground], and the chin and jaws being supported by the palms of each hand. The knees are just not touching the ground. Another tradition recommends putting all the weight on the elbows and shins of the feet, but in our tradition it is a little different and that [practice] is not in accordance with ours. The purpose [of this posture] is by making enough wind to move, it stops desire and anger. It also increases your strength, like an elephant. Externally, the [visions of the] complete *Buddha*-fields arise. Internally, meditative experiences and realizations arise simultaneously.

Nirmāṇakāya posture 138

Third, the *nirmāṇakāya* posture is like a crouching *rishi*. Put the soles of the feet on the ground with the body crouching. Draw in the knees by wrapping the elbows around them. The knees touch the chest, and the hands wrap around them. Straighten the spine. The neck is a little retracted. Next, place both elbows on top of the knees with the palms of the right and left hands touching [and supporting] the jaws (139). One of these body postures is enough. The purpose [of this posture] is that it serves as the agent for bringing and developing warmth, and it calms all of the coarse and subtle conceptual thoughts. Externally, the *nirmāṇakāya* visions arise. Internally, you generate special clear visions.

With any of these postures, respectively, do not hold them too tight, or try to make them too loose, and through that you will not encounter any hindrances and will generate great benefit of the positive qualities.

Other than these, there is the duck posture and the antelope posture.[12] The duck posture [entails] moving side to side. This posture seems convenient for beginners to encounter the visions in the expanse. Place the right elbow on the ground with the right palm [of the hand] supporting the side of the face, both legs with the knees bent a little, and with the calves stacked [on top of each other]. The purpose is that the winds fit into the central channel, so that an incredible magical display

---

12. The antelope posture is not explained in the text.

[of visions] arises. There is a significant increase in the visions in the expanse (140).

2.3.2.1.1.2 **Speech** 140

Second, the essential point of speech is described in the *rTags tshad sgron ma* [*Lamp of the Full Measure of the Signs*], "If you do not permanently cut off speech you won't be able to see the inexpressible truth, and the one great sphere of interconnectedness will not directly manifest." According to this passage, converse much less [than usual], and ultimately let go of all expressions, cut off speech, and stay [in silence].

2.3.2.1.1.3 **Mind** 140

Third, the essential point of mind is that so-called "mind" in its very essence is awakened awareness and this is in accordance with the gaze. Through focusing penetratingly on outside space, this makes the movements of the winds calm. Then, the profound enlightened intention of the inseparable pair—vast expanse and lively awakened awareness—will arise from this state. The previous [text] also says, "If you do not focus awakened awareness with the eye-gaze, this very awakened awareness will not directly manifest."

2.3.2.1.2 **The Essential Point of the [Eye] Gateways** 140

Second, the essential point of the [eye] gateways. Because primordial wisdom does not arise through any ordinary way of looking, you must [hold] the eye-[gaze] in accordance with the posture. These [three] gazes are done in accordance with the three sitting postures [described above]. In the *gSer gyi phreng ba* [*Golden Rosary*] it says, "In the *dharmakāya* posture the gaze looks upward. In the *nirmāṇakāya* posture (141) the gaze looks downward. In the *sambhogakāya* posture the gaze looks to one side or the other." According to this passage, the essential point of the [eye]-gateways is that there are certainly three ways of gazing, but the main point is meeting with the reality [of the visions] in the expanse. In the previous [text] it also says, "Gaze undistractedly with the eyes squinting slightly downward just below [the eyebrow boundary] of the sun." According to this passage, with the eyes squinting half open—neither too open nor too closed —look toward a site at a distance of an elbow length without [direct] contact with the sun. This is the essential point of looking. By mastering the essential point of the gateways, however long you focus on the object, you are able to do it.

2.3.2.1.3 The Essential Point of the Object [of Vision] 141

Third, in a high, elevated place, free of all adverse conditions, look through the fluid eye lamps at the distinctly bright, clear and pure sky, free of clouds, and the visions of clear-light will arise. Beginners should practice both early in the morning and late in the afternoon. When awakened awareness in this expanse is free from the eyebrow boundary, look to the clear sky. In the *mThing shogs* [*The Dark Blue Paper*] it says, "Look to the sovereignty of the *Nāgas* [west] in the early morning. Look to the place of the *Gandharvas* [east] in the early evening." According to this passage, look into the sky (142) in the west in the early morning, and the east in the early evening.

2.3.2.1.4 The Essential Point of Slowing Down the Winds and Awakened Awareness 142

Fourth, the essential point of slowing down the winds and awakened awareness. Some have taught that this has four wind practices [inhaling, inhaling a second time, holding, and exhaling], but this occurs through not understanding the essential point. According to the way the instructions [are given here], the wind isn't exhaled from the nose. From the mouth, inhale and exhale very slowly, the lips and teeth just not touching. Through relying on slowing the wind, this is called holding the mind as a prisoner. Through naturally purifying all the coming and going of the wind, these dissolve in the radiant essence of awakened awareness in the heart. [Ordinary] conceptual thoughts become self-calm and bare; empty awakened awareness directly arises.

2.3.2.2 Four Winds of Emanation—the Four Special Channels 142

Second, there are four winds of emanation that are activated and elevated. As this passage implies, there are four special great channels.

Everything is activated by these winds and all appearances of the seemingly existing world rise up by them. All the clear-light visions are activated through four special channels. The meditative experiences become directly manifest in the *dharmadhātu*, rise up, and increase more and more. In the *Thig le drug* [*Six Energy Drops*] it says, "In general, four things come together to make the aggregates [of the physical body] (143). The channels become like a matrix. There are four operational channels." According to this passage, there are four channels: the great golden *kati* channel, the white silk filament channel, the subtle coiled channel, and the crystal tube channel. According to this passage, the great golden *kati* channel, abiding in the heart, connects the heart to the center of the central channel. In the center of the heart, the heart-essence of radiant clear-light supports the complete [peaceful] assembly of the g.Yung drung [eternal swastika *Buddha* family]. [From there the channel goes to the] Brahma aperture where the wrathful deities [abide]. [The branches] of this radiant channel serve as a support for all kinds of energy drops that arise.

The interior of the [second] channel is like white silk filaments. [It extends from the heart] as one channel upward, like the Tibetan vowel *e*, and divides into two channels, where one side connects to the right eye. This channel serves as a support for engaging external objects. The other side [branch channel] connects to the Brahma aperture where it serves as a support for the arising of the essence of emptiness/radiance, the great awakened awareness, absent of all conceptual thought. When this reaches full measure, it serves as a support for the arising of the five or nine energy drops that stack up in the [interior tube of the upper central channel].

The third, the subtle coiled channel is from [the central channel at the heart down to the base] and then rises up through the center of the four *chakras* [navel, heart, throat, and crown] and joins to the left eye. It serves as a support for the arising of visions of the natural clear-light that directly arise within you (144).

The fourth, the crystal tube channel, is connected from the heart to the eyes. It serves as a support for letting the visions appear in you and subside in you.

Great compassion, which is the radiance of awakened awareness, arises through the lung channels to the mind.

2.3.2.3 Four Fires of Balancing the Temperature [The Four Lamps] 144

Fourth, is what the parable called "the four emanating fires that balance the temperature" [or the four lamps]. According to the passage, this pertains to the four lamps. These four are: the lamp of the fluid eye-lamp of the extensive lasso; the lamp of the empty energy drops; the lamp of the very pure expanse; and the lamp of self-occurring sublime knowledge. These four lamps make really clear that whatever visions of the radiance of awakened awareness appear are the enlightened bodies in the *Buddha*-fields. The warmth of primordial wisdom is balanced in all [these lamps], and through that it brings about the ripening of the threefold embodiment of enlightenment on the path. For example, by means of the great fire of existence, the warmth is balanced across everything in the seemingly existing world. Through that, it brings about the ripening of all plants and annual crops. Likewise, these sacred pith instructions [on the lamps] are established internally [as the view]. Therefore, in the *Rig pa rtsal dbang* [*Influence of the Liveliness of Awakened Awareness*] it says, "The four kinds of lamps are the internal teachings." According to this passage, these [four] will be explained a little separately. Penetrate [the essential points] of the body postures and the gazes [as previously described] (145). [First,] is the fluid eye lamp of the extensive lasso. Through focusing on the clear domain of space outside, initially a radiant light of very pure dark blue color appears. From that, what unfolds is made clear as the radiant colors of the five lights, much like a silk brocade. These are made clear as clear-light inside [even though they are seen] outside. In the *gSer gyi zhun* [*Refined Gold*] it says, "In the empty expanse of external space you will directly see the clear-light of the [internal] heart [lamp]. These are colored white, yellow, blue, red, and green, and smoke-colored." Some say that this passage refers to the expanse of the external sky and the external expanse is only referring to a cloudless sky. [However], the [ordinary] sky is not what is being referred to here. There is no connection between the person and this space. For that reason, the lamp follows whether the person is there or not. The open sky is just [a metaphor for] the basis of arising, but is not the real expanse. The internal sky, radiantly blue, when it arises outside, is what is referred to as the "[real] expanse of space." In the *gSer gyi phreng ba* [*Golden Rosary*] it says, "In the midst of the pure expanse of the external sky (146) the lamp of the internal expanse purifies." According to this passage, herein is an explanation about what is referred to as "the external expanse and the internal expanse." It is said to open what is not clear to be clear as an encirclement of rainbows. It doesn't mean that appearance has any dualistic outside and inside.

The lamp of the expanse is referred to as "the lamp of the empty energy drops." This is illustrated by those [masters] who [in front of a student, throw] a stone into a pond of water, so there are concentric ripples [spreading from where the stone was thrown]. The visions of the five lights at their perimeters are like this. [These visions] come in part from having purified the karmic winds.

Then, through having mastered the gaze of the extensive lasso, the bright lucidity of awakened awareness internally will increase. The visions are experienced as objectless and bare. This is the essence of "the lamp of self-occurring sublime knowledge."

Then, sublime knowledge of the object and the knowing of these objects is sharp and quick, and the [true] meaning of these words arises immediately in the domain of space. This is the liveliness of this. Then, awakened awareness that sees beyond appears as visions like swastikas one after the other, pearls strung together, or like floating golden threads. This is called "the radiance of sublime knowledge." [These visions] are [all of] the same essence (147) but from a certain point of view seem different.

2.3.2.4 The Golden Earth and Eight Clear Mirrors 147

Fourth, the parable says, "[All] have their place in the golden earth." The explanation of this passage is that the place of [liveliness of] awakened awareness is this very expanse. There is an increase in the radiant five-colored lights [arising] from the dark blue expanse. Real awakened awareness is inside the heart, but because it is made clear as external radiance, it is called "awakened awareness's [liveliness]." The visions of these [colored lights] are interlinked. From the perspective of dwelling inside and appearing outside, it is called "the essence of awakened awareness" and "awakened awareness that sees beyond." Through the words, "the basis of golden earth," in the expanse, all appearances that arise externally are the internal radiance of awakened awareness, therefore this teaching illustrates that this practice is free of [distinctions like] good/bad or stopping something/making something happen.

2.3.2.5 Four Great Rivers [Four Levels of Visions] 147

Fifth, the parable says, "four great rivers are the continuous flow of his merit." This passage refers to the four [levels of] visions. These are described in the *sPros bral rigs pa'i rtsal dbang* [*Influence of the Liveliness of Awakened Awareness Free of Elaboration*]: "[First,] the visions directly manifest in the *dharmadhātu*. [Second,] the meditative experiences of the visions increase. [Third], the visions reach the full measure of awakened awareness. [Finally], the visions come to an end as *dharmadhātu* exhaustion." According to this passage, these [stages] become distinguished as a function of becoming more familiar with them, like in the lower [vehicle] stages. It seems that the way of what is to be purified and the result of purification has been taught [to occur] as four levels (147). The difference between the quick path and the slow path is like one who travels in the sky or by land.

[First Level of Visions] 148

Then, the first [level of visions]. As taught, these visions directly appear in the *dharmadhātu*. Through having previously penetrated the four essential points as explained previously, there is the initial seeing of patterns of rainbows, which is the radiance/expanse of the essence of the *Sugatas* in your heart. The lamp of the empty energy drops is like a sphere of light. These [visions] arise, either clear or clouded, associated with coming and going, like three connected spheres of energy drops, and so forth. In between these, like the sun and its rays that appear as interlinked swastikas, is awakened awareness that sees beyond. The essence of awakened awareness is the inexpressible radiance of emptiness/clarity. This is like the reflection of a face in a mirror. You should know it is the same nature with real internal awakened awareness.

Therefore, if you do not know this, through grasping them as solid with conceptual thought, awakened awareness [dualistically seems] to radiate inward and appear outward. Then, in that becoming a hindrance, you make the mistake of reifying these interlinked visions. For that reason, awakened awareness relies upon the essential point of the channels. The signs of liberation are such that subtle [energy drops] are interlinked and at angular patterns (149). Having relied upon these energy drops, the signs of liberation are such that in the corners of the angles there are subtle energy drops joined as pairs. Having relied upon the essential point of the winds, the signs of liberation are such that you do not engage [these visions] as having coming and going, and you should engage the expanse and the energy drops at the fence [of the eyebrows] like a master.

In the *Thog 'bebs* [*Falling Lightning Bolt*], it says, "Practice skillfully, which is the essential point of [practicing with] the inseparable pair-- skillful means and sublime knowledge." According to this passage, the essential point of the object in the daytime is the sublime knowledge of relying upon the [expanse] of *dharmakāya*, using the sun and a magnifying glass. In the evening is the skillful means relying upon the *sambhogakāya* using the moon and the water crystal. In both the early morning and early evening is the pair [means and knowledge] of relying on the *nirmāṇakāya* using fire, and so forth. First, rely on looking by just about touching [the fire, i.e., by being very close]. Through having become more familiar with this, the light of these visions will become more and more clear, and their movement will become more and more stable. The winds and the mind, which slow down at the three gateways, become self-calm. Internally, you will [begin to have] special meditative experiences and realizations. Because of that, you are generating a sublime knowledge better than before about the words [of the instructions] and their meaning. Through that, you will attain one-third of the influence of primordial wisdom. At this time, if hindrances occur [and you die], you are assured a place in the naturally emanating after-death *bardo* (150).

In the *rTag sgron ma* [*Lamps of the Signs*] it says, "If you die at the time the expanse is free from the eyebrow fence, at that time it is said you will be reborn in the naturally emanating *Buddha*-fields, and the proliferation of the [third level] visions and meditative experiences start, but it is the [last one], the direct endpoint of the visions. Therefore, realize this as the same. For that reason, not by seeing just the first signs of the visions from the expanse, but through having become familiar with [awakened] awareness internally, this is the essential point of unifying the expanse and [the liveliness of] awakened awareness. In the *rTags sgron bu* [*Minor Text of the Lamp of Signs*] it says, "By mixing the expanse and [the liveliness of] awakened awareness, you will be reborn in the naturally emanating realms."

[Second Level of Visions—Proliferation] 150

Second, the proliferation of the previous visions as meditative experiences. Through practicing meditation as previously described [in the first level], the expanse and the [liveliness of] awakened awareness [in the form of the visions] is sometimes clear and sometimes not clear. At times the visions proliferate, and the expanse and awakened awareness separate from the eyebrow boundary. The five lights of the five primordial wisdoms come [straight] upwards [from the eyebrow boundary], like spokes and squares, or in the form of felt. Sometimes the visions seem as large as a country. There are visions of colors. [Visions are] in the form of eyes in a net, a web, a bouquet of flowers (151), and the symbols of the *Buddha* families or their celestial places. These are the visions of [various] shapes. This is called "the development of light from space." These visions are also like *stupas*, hooks, tridents, arrows, spear-heads, and so forth. This is called "the development of primordial wisdom from the expanse." These ornaments [coming] from the expanse complete the full measure [of these visions]. This is also the lamp of the energy drops. The visions gradually proliferate [and increase in size] from about the size of a pea to the size of a shield. Then, on the circumference of the five lights, visions [in the form of] spheres arise. This is awakened awareness's [liveliness] developing. This is called "concentrating the quintessential vital essence."

2.3.2.6 All the Stars and Planets 152

In the *Awakened Awareness of the Cuckoo* it says, "All the stars and planets shine from his waist." Deciphering this passage, the words are explained accordingly: [All the visions are] interconnected to awakened awareness. They quickly fly by like a bird; or they seem to run like a deer through the rock faces of the mountains; or then they move very slowly like the [mythical creature, the] *sharana* [like a slowly crawling slug]. Finally, they move very slowly much like a honey bee hovering over a flower.

To summarize briefly, their stability depends on how much you are familiar with this, so that the visions of light become full blown, and awakened awareness becomes much more stable, and at the endpoint, wherever you look, the entire world is filled with visions of clear-light (152). Through that, [the visions] stay without wavering.

When these clear-light visions become wide-spread and are just like felt, the essential point of the gazes is described in the *Zhang zhung snyan rgyud* [*Oral Transmission from Zhang Zhung*]. It says, "When the visions are seen semi-circular and predominately white, the essential point is to look upward. When the visions are seen upright and predominately red, the essential point is to look downward. When the visions are seen as squares and predominately yellow, the essential point is to look to the right. When the visions are seen as round and predominately green, the essential point is to look to the left. When the visions are seen as triangular and predominately blue, look to the side and center. When all five forms [squares, etc.] are present and are about the size of a house, see them as equal." According to this passage, at the time primordial wisdom is about the size of a house, don't change the sitting posture.

If the energy drops do not proliferate, focus the eyes in the center [of this space] and this will stabilize the channels and the light. If the splendor of the light fades, focus [the mind] in the intermediate space. If thought becomes activated, hold the wind and exhale. The essential point of the expanse is to concentrate on the center [of that space] and look guiding the eyes to the side. The essential point of awakened awareness (153) is to focus on the inter-connected [visions] in the space. At the time of seeing the embodiment of enlightenment, the essential point for completing that is to look unchangingly at its radiance. That is the essential point. As the meditative experiences start to increase, free from hindrances, the full measure comes from having freed the expanse and the [liveliness of] awakened awareness from the eyebrow boundary, and through that, by uniting the four-fold visions of primordial wisdom, liberation comes.

If the visions arise in the form of squares then you will be liberated from aggregates [of visions]. If the visions in the expanse arise as an array of spheres adorned with a four-petalled lotus, you will become liberated at the very moment the clear-light arises. In brief, if the shapes and colors of the visions are completed, and the hindrances also become liberated by the visions being spontaneously present, then you will turn back [saṁsāra] in the bardo of rebirth. That is the enlightened intention of the mothers [ḍākinīs] of the lamps. At the time that the energy drops appear about the size of leather shields, you get the full measure of the energy drops. It is uncertain whether they get bigger than this. Each of these energy drops has five colors of light around the perimeter, and when the single enlightened body of the deity appears, this is reaching the endpoint of the meditative experiences of these visions. This is the end of proliferation of the visions.

[Third Level of Visions—Reaching Full Measure] 153

Third, the visions [of the liveliness of] awakened awareness reaching full measure. The profound essential point of this path is for you to remain in the fundamental nature of awakened awareness (154) and bound to the primordial completion of the three-fold embodiment of enlightenment. Through that, at the time that the visions reach full measure, you reach the fruition, the endpoint of what you have aspired to—all of the positive qualities of awakened awareness, the truth of the path of the maṇḍala of the enlightened completion bodies, and all of the [32] major [and 83] minor marks, without exception. These [marks] are not on the body, but complete the skill of the visions of the path. This is the reason this path of natural Great Completion is magnificent. Therefore, the aspect of increasing the positive qualities of awakened awareness becomes stronger, and you will have mastered the five primordial wisdoms in the expanse, and because of that, in the midst of the arising of the group of five [one in the center and four around it] energy drops, the *nirmāṇakāya* arises, which comes from reaching the endpoint of the practice. It arises from a half of the enlightened body until a full, single enlightened body arises. When the primordial wisdom of the *sambhogakāya* reaches full measure, the *Buddhas* of the five *Buddha* families, Kun snang and so forth, arise from a single enlightened body, with their full ornaments, up until arising with their consorts. From the pure practice of the *dharmakāya* occurring, the different *maṇḍalas* of the principal deities and their surrounding retinues along the perimeter become clear (155). In the *Thog 'bebs* [*Falling Lightning Bolt*], it says, "The sign that the development has reached full measure is that the enlightened bodies complete with all their ornaments are made clear."

2.3.2.7 Five Radiant Lamps Generated from the Crown 155

Furthermore, in the *Rig pa khu byug* [*Awakened Awareness of the Cuckoo*] it says, "The five radiant lamps are generated from the crown of the head." This passage illustrates that at the time the visions of the [liveliness of] awakened awareness increase and reach full measure, the five primordial wisdoms become fully manifest. At that time the external visions reach full measure, because the solidness of the visions self-dissolves, and through that, emptiness primordial wisdom directly becomes manifest. At the full measure of seeing, the appearance of this immense clear-light is limitless, and through that, mirror-like primordial wisdom directly becomes manifest. Whatever arises is self-appearing and even, without distinctions, and free from dualistic seeing, and through that, sameness primordial wisdom directly becomes manifest. The physical body has reached full measure. All the visions of the *Buddha*-fields of five victorious *Buddha* families appear; from the heart of all these clear enlightened bodies, light concentrated into five light-rays occur, and having penetrated the center of your own heart, you become connected to it. From the hair tuft [at the third eye point], a full arm's length of rays of light come, and through that the winds of primordial wisdom (156) elevate five or nine stacked energy drops about the size of a basin.

At the Brahma aperture, the radiance of clear bliss of the eighty flaming *maṇḍalas* of the wrathful deities arises, and inside the heart, the *maṇḍalas* of the assembly of the forty-five peaceful deities arise everywhere, and all the assembly of the eternal, completely accomplished deities arises. Because the radiance of primordial wisdom is made clear in all the subtle light channels, throughout all the pores, and at the sites of each of the coarse and subtle particles [of the body], immeasurable *Buddha*-fields become self-clear without mixing [in each other], and by knowing this, discriminating primordial wisdom directly becomes manifest.

The mind reaches full measure, and through that, the ordinary mind with unceasing conceptual thought, and the sense-mind, and the sense consciousnesses subside; and from that, self-awakened awareness directly manifests. When the mind enters matter it moves [that matter, i.e., psychokinesis]. You will come to know the minds of others, and so forth. There are six paranormal abilities, and you will see beyond into immeasurable *Buddha*-fields of the Victorious Ones and their refuge objects. You will get the power of immeasurable gateways of sublime knowledge and *samādhi*, and through that, all-accomplishing primordial wisdom (157) directly becomes manifest.

In brief, through purifying the solidness of the physical body, the channels, and winds become self-purified, and the collection [of the physical body, channels and winds] is immediately dismantled. The direct and coarse connection between mind and body is reversed. The subtle [substantiality of the body] and awakened awareness together are latent, and [the body] sometimes [and sometimes does not] arise to the mind. When it arises it sees the aspect of the appearance of *saṁsāra*, and therefore, it is called "grasping the aspect of both *saṁsāra* and *nirvāṇa*." Through [the residual substantiality of the body] disappearing in the expanse, like a shooting star, the continuation of [all ripening] karmic actions and habitual karmic tendencies disappears. At this time, it is called "completing the three-fold embodiment of enlightenment as the path of visions."

2.3.2.8 Three Secret Seed-Syllables are Set in Mind 157

Eighth, in the *Rig pa khu byug* [*Awakened Awareness of the Cuckoo*] it says, "Three secret seed syllables manifest as the enlightened heart-mind." According to this passage, this refers to the enlightened beings in the

Buddha-fields of the *Tathāgatas* and [all] the positive qualities of primordial wisdom. Here, they directly appear at the [purified] sense-gateways. This is only found in natural Great Completion, not in some other path. Therefore, it should be secret. By uttering the three seed syllables, below the primordial gShen[13] [vehicle], the three-fold embodiment of enlightenment reaches the endpoint and comes to fruition, and here [in Great Completion] it is called "fulfilled (158) as the enlightened heart-mind." It arises at the appearance of path [not fruition] enlightenment.

Here, some have asserted that the empty forms are deluded visions. Some have asserted that these are ultimate truth. Neither is correct. These [visions] are a kind of self-radiance of the *Tathāgatas*, and because of that are not deluded. Because these arise externally as the radiance of awakened awareness, they are like reflections [in a mirror], and ultimately there is no reason to take them as real. Because these are the essence of self-radiance, for that reason, [all] external appearances are exhausted.

[Fourth Level of Vision—*Dharmadhātu* Exhaustion] 158

Fourth, the visions of *dharmadhātu* exhaustion. By relying on this profound essential point, the increase in primordial wisdom moved by the winds reaches full measure and appears like the moon that begins to wane. Their decrease reaches the zero-point, and so forth. All the visions of clear-light in the *dharmadhātu* have dissolved in the expressionless expanse. Because nothing whatsoever appears, it is called "exhaustion." Their ultimate truth is like the moon of a new moon day. Even if something appears, it is like there is nothing increasing or decreasing.

At the time the visions increase, they don't get bigger, (159) and at the time they are diminishing, they don't become smaller. At the beginning the light was thumb-sized; it never got bigger and smaller. It is called "not getting full and not diminishing."

With respect to the manner of exhaustion, it comes gradually or instantaneously. Exhaustion [gradually] comes from having reached the full measure of the four [levels of] visions. Exhaustion also comes instan-

---

13. Ye gshen: the name of the primordial Buddha at the eighth stage of the Nine Ways of Bon.

taneously in the following way: through becoming familiar with directly seeing them increasing in the *dharmadhātu*, as was previously the case, the visions reach full measure, no longer develop, and become exhausted. That [experience pertains to] those of best capacity, but that occurs for very few. However, at the time of exhaustion [of the visions], externally there is the exhaustion of the visions of the five lights, now endowed with the enlightened bodies; and internally there is the exhaustion of the phenomena of the sense-organs, now as the illusory body; and secretly, there is the exhaustion of the all conceptual thoughts of the [ordinary] mind. The solidness of the external objects and the physical body have reached full measure and become exhausted. All the aspects of the universal ground subsumed under the mind, and all that is endowed with the subtle karmic seeds of habitual karmic tendencies, become exhausted. The essential point is that external appearances should come to exhaustion, and having become freed of the winds that move awakened awareness, the internal essence should be stable in the expanse. If these are not exhausted, you won't be able to become liberated from the three realms (160). At the time of exhaustion, the radiance of awakened awareness arises and the karmic winds are exhausted at the same time. The winds of primordial wisdom remain inside the expanse and co-emerge.

2.3.2.8.1 The Two Attainments 160

At this time the two attainments occur.

2.3.2.8.1.1 Free of Re-Birth

Because of having attained control over rebirth, if you serve the welfare of sentient beings, when gradually over time [the visions] dissolve, the five fingers of the hand appear as if [each is] covered with light. By focusing on that, deluded appearances dissipate naturally, and seeing the support and what is supported of the container and its contents becomes like a water-moon.

2.3.2.8.1.2 Great Consciousness-Transference

Your own physical body also appears without inherent nature like reflections in a mirror. This is called, "the arising of the enlightened embodiment of the Great Consciousness-Transference [Rainbow Body]." Then, you qualify for the same status as the first twenty-four masters of the rainbow body [awareness-holder lineage]. This kind of body-holder is such that others with impure eyes see it [your body] as substantial, but to you, your body also appears transparent. In an instant, if you want you could make your body invisible [to others].

Tapihritsa [was able to appear] in whatever way was suitable. sMe phyug [g.yung drung rGyal mtshan][14] gave a name to Lord Tapihritsa as the boy called rNyed legs ["happy to be found"]. It was said that when he asked [the boy] to do something the boy immediately disappeared. Likewise, there is another story that explains that Lung bon Lhag nyen tried to visit a person, Tshe dbang Rig 'dzin (161). Sometimes the two met human to human, and then they both disappeared with no one knowing where they had gone. At that time by inconceivable, immeasurable enlightened activities, direct and indirect, they served the benefit immeasurably of the six classes of beings. You should know the ways of the highest enlightened intention and conduct of the famous [*yogi*], Dran pa Nam mkha'. Especially, by engaging his awakened awareness toward three thousand human beings, all of them were able to purify their elements and achieve *Buddhahood*. How he mastered engaging [awakened awareness in the service of others] comes from the time he [achieved] the form of an enlightened [rainbow] body. If he couldn't serve the great welfare of others, how could these three-thousand human beings have been immediately liberated? His fingers and toes appeared to him covered with light. From that very moment, internally, he engaged in the expanse, and externally, all the appearances had turned back [from being substantial], and through that there is the edge [of reaching rainbow body]. There was no [need for him to] focus on the light-like fingers and limbs, but only keep his focus on the visions in the expanse. Through that, the physical body and the radiance of appearance dissolved into the expanse internally, and awakened awareness coiled inside of the expanse. Without being separated from or united to the enlightened bodies and primordial wisdoms, he stayed in the essence of the youthful vase body (162).

---

14. sMe is the family name. *phyugs po* implies a wealthy family.

The way to do the deed of emptying *saṁsāra* through enlightened activity in the two enlightened form-bodies is described in the *dByings rig rin po che'i mdzod* [*Precious Treasury of the Expanse and Awakened Awareness*], where I explain it in greater detail.

2.3.2.9 Final Support—Four Seasons and Four Queens 162

[In the *Awakened Awareness of the Cuckoo*] it says, "The four queens of the [respective] four seasons." This passage refers to the final support. The four final supports are described in the *gSer gyi zhun* [*Refined Gold*] where it says, "[The first] are the three immovable bases. [The second] are holding full measure with the three stabilities. [The third] is to set the nails with the three attainments. [The fourth] is to show the full measure of liberation with the four confidences. This passage describes these four.

2.3.2.9.1 The Three Immovable Bases 162

First, the three immovable bases:

(1) Because of making the body posture immovable, the channels and winds settle down by themselves.

(2) By not moving from the gazes with the eyes, the visions greatly increase.

(3) By not moving the mind and keeping expressionless, you enter into the unification of the expanse and [the liveliness of] awakened awareness.

2.3.2.9.2 The Three Stabilities 162

Second, the three stabilities:

(1) Through the stability of the physical body remaining without any activity, all activity is purified in its own place.

(2) Through the stability wherein the winds settle down by themselves, you end the conditions that move conceptual thought.

(3) Through the stability wherein the visions are without agitation or fluttering, the *Buddha*-fields (163) reach full measure.

At that very moment [there are two effects]:

(1) the arising in the three gateways, and

(2) assessment of dreams.

2.3.2.9.2.1 Signs Arising in the Three Gateways 163
The first of the signs is after the direct manifestation of *dharmadhātu*.

[The Four Signs]

2.3.2.9.2.1.1 Signs Directly Manifest in the Dharmadhātu

2.3.2.9.2.1.1.1 The Three Gates

2.3.2.9.2.1.1.1.1 **Body** 163
The physical body becomes like a tortoise in a basin that remains immovable. It occurs through its interdependence with the [winds] moving slowly in the channels. When Great Completion meditation is free of doing, the nails are set on the limbs [through the posture], and through that, all activity is purified in its own way, and self-occurring primordial wisdom free of all doing arises.

2.3.2.9.2.1.1.1.2 **Speech** 163
Regarding speech, without speaking you become like a mute person. This comes from consciousness penetrating the interior of the channels. Being free of the very basis of expression, the nail is set on speech, and through that the basis of expression goes beyond *saṁsāra*, and only enlightened speech arises from a state of unceasing primordial wisdom.

2.3.2.9.2.1.1.1.3 **Mind** 163
The mind is like a bird flying in the sky caught in a cage. Likewise, holding it in its own place occurs from mixing awakened awareness and clear-light. By setting the nail of self-liberation free of grasping on the visions as mind, as a result all elaboration toward sense objects becomes self-purified.

2.3.2.9.2.1.2 At the Time Previous Meditative Experiences Increase 163

(164) The second [sign] is at the time the meditative experiences [of the visions] are increasing. The physical body is like a person suffering from an illness, who is without any shame. This occurs from when the winds enter into the central channel.

Through having set the nail in general on the body, free of the very basis of doing, the physical body, which is the basis of doing, goes beyond suffering, and the enlightened body arises in the state of unborn primordial wisdom.

[Ordinary] speech, whatever is said, is like the spontaneous utterances of a madman and comes from primordial wisdom that never stays in the same place. By setting the nail on all expressed words free of recognizing them [by a self], indeterminate primordial wisdom arises in its own way.

The [ordinary] mind is like a person who has become intoxicated with poison. As such there is little gathering or elaboration [of conceptual thought]. [Its movement] comes from the unborn liveliness of awakened awareness. By setting the nail on all [ordinary] mindfulness [and conceptual thought] in the unborn state, they become self-liberated. Mindfulness and conceptual thought, free of grasping, become self-purified, and disappear by themselves.

2.3.2.9.2.1.3 At the Time Awakened Awareness Reaches Full Measure 164

Third, at the time awakened awareness reaches full measure, the physical body is like an elephant stuck in a mud [pool] that comes out by its own power [when it wants to]. Likewise, because this [path] is completed without effort, and [the realization] comes from its own power, by setting the nail on activities of the body as unobstructed, (165) all-accomplishing primordial wisdom comes of its own power.

Speech is like the [melodious] song of a child demon, who completely engages another's ears with whatever is sung. This comes from having established the power of primordial wisdom's compassion. By setting the nail on expressed speech, whatever is expressed is unobstructed primordial wisdom, and self-occurring primordial wisdom, free from what is to be expressed, arises.

The mind is like a person who had and was cured of smallpox and never gets it again. Likewise, once [ordinary conceptual thought] self-disappears it never comes back after that, and with some familiarity, mastery will come. By setting the nail on the sense-mind that is the agent of mindfulness that acts moment-by-moment, primordial wisdom that totally calms [thought] elaboration is brought into its own power.

2.3.2.9.2.1.4 At the Time of Dharmadhātu Exhaustion 165

Fourth, at the time of *dharmadhātu* exhaustion, the physical body is like a dead person in a charnel ground who has no fear. This occurs from the [ordinary] mind getting caught up in the net of clear-light. By setting the nail on the fixation point endowed with fearlessness and confidence, the sign of the effortless mind, free of all effort, arises (166), going beyond suffering in the domain of eternal space.

Speech is like a kind of echo that repeats [the original sound] out there afterwards. It comes from penetrating the seed-syllables, winds, and energy drops that abide in the channels. By setting the nail on the mind of expressionless self-liberation, primordial wisdom, free of grasping expressions, arises in its own way.

The mind is like the mist that in an instant self-disappears. It comes from *saṁsāra* self-vanishing. By setting the nail on the mind's non-deluded primordial wisdom, the basis of mindfulness that goes beyond the mind becomes the enlightened heart-mind, and you remain in a state of non-deluded primordial wisdom.

The four signs of the physical body occur from definitely attaining the four influences of the basis. The four [signs] of speech occur from definitely attaining the four influences of the path. The four signs of the sense-mind occur from directly manifesting the four influences of the fruition.

2.3.2.9.2.2 Assessment of Dreams 166

Second, assessment of the full measure of dreams. By the stages of diligence, the best practitioners disrupt dreaming so that the clear-light of deep sleep arises. [Such a practitioner] definitely attains enlightenment [rainbow body] in this very lifetime (167). Middling practitioners, through recognizing the dream as a dream [while dreaming], are able to voluntarily transform the dream, and will become enlightened in the after-death *bardos*. Lesser capacity practitioners, through having disrupted the negative habitual karmic propensities of dreaming, have only good dreams, and give up their last breath in the innate emanation *Buddha*-fields.

2.3.2.9.2.3 **The Three Attainments** 167

Third, the three attainments have three divisions. In the *gSer gyi zhun* [*Refined Gold*] it says,

"(1) Through having mastered these very visions, all conditions arise as friends to the visions.

(2) Through having mastered the physical body, the body no longer appears as solid but as clear-light.

(3) Through having mastered the secret winds and mind, conceptual thought subsides in the expanse." So it is said.

2.3.2.9.2.4 **The Four Confidences** 167

Fourth, the four confidences:

(1) [The first is that] after hearing about the positive qualities of enlightenment, you are free of both the expectation of attaining it and the fear of not attaining it.

(2) [Second], you have made the determination that there isn't even the smallest hair tip of *Buddhahood* existing on its own other than your own awakened awareness.

(3) [Third], you have heard about the extended suffering of the three lower realms, and remain free of either the expectation of not falling into them or the fear of falling into them.

(4) [Fourth], you have made a determination that by having self-awakened awareness primordially, you will not be reborn, and there is never any agent that [makes you] wander in *saṁsāra* ever again (168).

2.3.2.9.2.5 The Four Servants Acting to Serve Him 168

[In the *Awakened Awareness of the Cuckoo*] it says, "The four servants acting to serve him." According to this passage, this refers to four [kinds of] sublime knowledge.

(1) [First], is the ability to make discriminations about all the unmixed phenomena [of the world] with more discriminating sublime knowledge.

(2) [Second], is the ability [to know] how all phenomena are subsumed under self-awakened awareness with the sublime knowledge that gathers [and inter-connects] everything.

(3) [Third], is making a determination that all phenomena are self-liberated with the sublime knowledge that brings about complete liberation.

(4) [Fourth], is bringing about the production of all phenomena in the expanse, wherein nothing whatsoever exists, except for the original purity of self-awakened awareness, with the sublime knowledge that completely produces everything.

Thus, the *yogi* who takes hold of the instructions endowed with the forty-two essential points of by-passing [practice] instantly self-purifies the deluded appearances of *saṁsāra*. [Such a *yogi* knows] that the innate basis of original purity is in its own place, and awakened awareness stably exists there. There is no doubt.

2.4 Consciousness-Transference and After-Death Bardo Practices 168

The meaning of the third [section] refers to the instructions for liberation in the after-death *bardos* for those of middling capacity while in the dying process, and while in the *bardo* of the *dharmadhātu*. This has three divisions—the normal [life] *bardo*, the dying process *bardo*, and the *bardo* of the *dharmadhātu*.

2.4.1 *Bardo* of [Normal] Life 169

First (169), [the normal life *bardo*]. On the base of the original, spontaneously present universal ground, a deposit of habitual karmic tendencies establishes this [ground] as a storehouse consciousness of all previous afflictive emotions. For example, it is like a mirror covered with flecks of rust, so that from the beginning it is covered by stains. These become the seeds of future defilements generating future karmic afflictive emotions. Therefore, through the power of accumulating distinct karmic actions, you will be propelled by their force of suffering, happiness, and [a state] in between, in the [six] realms [of *saṁsāra*]. This is called "[karmic] power because it is the root of the ordinary deluded mind." Humans are especially caught up in the five physical aggregates, so that the appearance of the five embodiments of enlightenment becomes obscured. Through being bound to the elements and sense-experiences, the clear-light [is obscured]. Through being caught up in the experience of karmic [ripening], primordial wisdom and the visions of the *dharmadhātu* become obscured, and because of that you engage deluded appearance as "normal." Through that you are lead through suffering in your next life and thereafter. Therefore, the mind naturally becomes fearful of endless suffering, and from that you will aspire to become emancipated.

On this path initially you must [listen to the teachings] and train the mind. Then, through having reflected on this, you must focus [in concentration]. Finally, through having meditated, you must rely upon direct realization (170). You must gain the confidence in your practices, so that you won't come back into *saṁsāra* again. As it says in the *gSer gyi zhun* [*Refined Gold*], "In the *bardo* of remaining in this normal life, in hearing, reflecting upon, and meditation on [the teachings], you must generate earnestness." So it is said.

2.4.2 *Bardo* of the Time of Dying 170

Second, is the *bardo* of the time of dying. A person of best capacity is like a small child who doesn't care about dying or not dying. They don't need these instructions. A person of middling capacity dies like a dog. Of them, the best are not harmed by objects and conditions, like [dying] on the road, a city, or crowded cross-road. Those of middling, middling capacity go to a cave, mountain, or desolate valley, or a place where they can't be seen. Those of lesser middling capacity are like a king dying. When he gets sick [attendants] use medicine and perform rituals. When dying, he is surrounded by relatives and friends. They shed tears. With his final suffering words he gives his last testament as he dies. Even after he dies they perform rituals: seven-day rituals, funerary rites, and so forth. The way of dying like this is the sign of not having the confidence of the practice of Great Completion.

This is not the right way of the *yogi* as meant here (171). It is the way of dying for those not established on this path. Therefore, the *yogi* who practices this path engages the embodiment of enlightenment and the primordial wisdoms. Those who engage the interior clear-light [at the time of death] remain in the sleeping lion posture, and their minds go through the pathways of the eyes, in a state of being free of emanating and gathering, [focused] on the ultimate truth of the inseparable pair of the expanse and [the liveliness of] awakened awareness. [Through such practice they] leave the formative aggregate of life, and at that instant become liberated. As previously described in the *gSer gyi zhun* [*Refined Gold*] it says, "In the *bardo* of the jaws of death, the elements are gathered. Being mindful, free of distraction, and clear is important. Take hold of the natural state with the instructions of the clear- light. Right now, meditative practice is like an escort to the dying process. The visions of the *bardo* are like a welcoming party. You are certain to become liberated at that very instant." According to this passage, right now focus the mind and the eyes on the clear sky, and mix the expanse [with the liveliness of] awakened awareness. After dying, while remaining in [the inseparable pair, lively] awakened awareness/expanse, consider, "I will surely set up my mind without a fixation point, and will exhale my last breath with the intention of going beyond suffering in the domain of unelaborated space." This is the sacred essential point (172).

At the time [of dying], those who necessarily rely on the [instructions] are given elaboration of the words, pointing out [the pair] awakened awareness/expanse by their lama or their spiritual brothers or sisters who have flawless spiritual duties. Engaging the object or place is similar to the pith instructions of transparent primordial wisdom. At the time they take their final breaths, they should express step-by-step twenty-one *HIG*s and through that imagine awakened awareness in the form [of a seed-syllable] *A;* and with each *HIG* [uttered it moves a distance of] a thumb-size [up the central channel] from the heart. From the Brahma aperture it goes very far up, and through that liberation comes. Furthermore, at this time, you have to engage these instructions on consciousness-transference to the *sambhogakāya*, which is covered under the middling [section] of the *Lam mngon sangs rgyas pa'i rgyud* [*Tantra of the Path of Directly Manifested Buddhahood*], and [develop] the meditative experiences. Those endowed with this kind of essential point, without relying on the stages of dying, in the way they [exhale their last] breaths and transfer their consciousnesses, reach *nirvāṇa*. Those who have these pith instructions but are not confident are like ordinary kinds of beings [at the time of death] (173).

The way of [the elements] dissolving has been taught extensively in *dByings rig rin po che'i mdzod* [*Precious Treasury of the Expanse and Awakened Awareness*] where it describes the gathering of the channel winds, the experience of the four external elements, of the five internal kinds of space, of the five secret life-forces, and the innermost secret twenty-one remaining winds dissolving.

Herein, the way the elements dissolve is easy to understand [even for] those of dull faculties. As described in the previous [in the *Refined Gold*] where it says, "When the earth element dissolves into earth, the physical body without exception becomes heavy and you do not eat. The strength of standing and walking is exhausted. When the water element dissolves into water, all the fluids flow from the mouth and nose by themselves. When fire dissolves into fire, the heat of the physical body is lost and is gathered from the extremities. When the wind element dissolves into wind, all the limbs shake when they move. At that point in time, the eyeballs turn upward. This is a preview of having gone beyond [i.e., having physically died]. It is important [at that time] to remember the instructions from your lama." Thus, according to this passage, all the blood from the smallest capillaries is made to gather at the life-force channel [in the heart]. Through that, one-by-one, three drops of blood drip [into the heart space], and through that, one-by-one come three long or short exhalations of the breath, and at the end, the external breath ceases. After that moment, in three stages—appearing, proliferating, and attaining—within three seconds, you will recall near-attainment. Through that, it becomes difficult to take hold of, and it [usually] comes as if becoming unconscious (174). Then, at the instant you become clear of [and awaken] from that, you will recognize that what has arisen is primordially established clear-light, like a cloudless sky, free of the liveliness of the visions, and free of all conceptual thought whatsoever. Through that, by holding the focus with awakened awareness straight into the originally pure expanse, enlightenment will come, as described in the *gSer gyi thur* [*Golden Spoon*] where it says, "This is the time that the ordinary mind is decreasing and primordial wisdom is increasing. At that very moment complete *Buddhahood* comes. You [have realized] the eternal unchanging [enlightenment]. *E ma ho!*"

2.4.3 *Bardo* of *Dharmadhātu* 174

Third, the *bardo* of *dharmadhātu*. If you have not become liberated in this previously described original purity like space as it arises, in what is called "dissolving into clear-light," awakened awareness emerges from the eye [lamps]. Through that, four moments of the near attainment of primordial wisdom arise thereafter. This [stage] is called "the basic vision of clear-light." In the open space, the clear-light and the self-radiance of the complete multi-colored five surrounding primordial wisdom [lights] arise, and through recognizing these as self-appearing, you become liberated. In the *Yang rtse* [*Epitome*] it says, "In this tradition, awakened awareness emerges from the eye [lamps]. In the openness of space, the light arises. Those who have these instructions at this point in time become liberated." If you have not become liberated from that, it is called "dissolving while united to the clear-light" (175). From these previous visions—ultimate sound, light, and light-rays—those who become familiar and acquainted with this will have the way of arising of the visions of the enlightened bodies. This is described in the *gZer bu* [*Twenty-One Nails*] where it says, "The light becomes the *Buddha*-fields without center or edges, like rainbows arising in the sky. Sound becomes an insubstantial roar in the domain of space. These [sounds] are self-occurring and continuous like a dragon's thunderous roar. Light-rays become an illuminated indeterminate magical display, like a silken or woolen brocade. For a person who is familiar and acquainted with this, the complete embodiment of enlightenment and the *Buddha*-fields will arise." According to this passage, at this point in time, the light-rays and complete enlightened bodies abiding in your own heart arise, connecting you to the enlightened heart-mind. In the *gSer zhun* [*Refined Gold*] it says, "Inside the heart is clear-light. This is the heart-essence of [the] heart and is thumb-sized. This light appears connecting with the embodiment of enlightenment. With respect to that, set up [the mind] staring without distraction." According to this passage, if you can hold your own mind on this light it is called "awakened awareness entering into the light." Then, you will be able to concentrate free of conceptual thought and naturally stay that way. Then, imagine all these visions dissolving into light-rays in the region of your own heart (176), and when you have that feeling, it is called "light dissolving into awakened awareness." Through recognizing that these visions are your own originally pure nature in their own place, you will become liberated by this very [realization]. If you do not become liberated in this [way, the next stage] is called "unification dissolving into wisdom." [At that time], a single. very fine filament of light [comes] from your own heart. By viewing how this penetrates space, the visions arise much more extensively. From the previous [text, *Refined Gold*] it says, "In having the vision of the physical body as light, at that point in time, primordial wisdom arises as the five forms of colors. At that time, you take hold of the essential point as being recognized by itself." According to this passage, you see these lights as blue, white, yellow, and red, and these four forms [of colors] as close but not touching [each other]. Additionally, each of these colors arises adorned with matching energy drops about the size of a mirror, and each of these [energy drops] is adorned with five smaller energy drops. On top of these [energy drops] are [surrounding colored] spheres of light arising like a parasol. If you are still not liberated in the expanse [at this time] it is called "the visions of the four primordial wisdoms united." In fact, if it arises according to the meaning of the passage, it arises as five forms of light, and these arise unobstructedly. These complete equally the visions of the five primordial wisdoms (177).

If [at this point in time] you do not know these as self-appearing, [the next stage] is called "primordial wisdom dissolving into spontaneous presence." The previous visions and awakened awareness are gathered into the spheres of light. It has the feeling of spheres of light gathering, whose manner of arising is the liveliness [of awakened awareness], and above that are originally pure visions like the sky purified of stains. Below that is the *maṇḍala* of the all-powerful wrathful deities. Below that is the complete *maṇḍala* of the g.Yung drung [eternal, peaceful deities and their] retinues, and in the cardinal directions are the naturally emanating *Buddha*-fields. Below that are the deities as emanations of sTon pa g.Shen rab who are subduing the appearances of the six realms. This is called "the appearance of the basis, wherein self-appearance does not move from the basis."

There are eight ways by which they arise.

2.4.3.1 **Eight Visions** 177

The way the eight visions appear:

(1) The first arises as great compassion. Through that, the power of compassion enters into *saṁsāra*, with no partiality to *saṁsāra* or *nirvāṇa*.

(2) The second pertains to visions arising as light, made clear internally as an aspect of appearing.

(3) The third, through these [visions now] arising as the embodiment of enlightenment, they are not divided into any [distinct] visions whatsoever.

(4) The fourth pertains to the visions arising and becoming transparent as primordial wisdom.

(5) The fifth, through these [visions] arising as non-dual, the mind stays one-pointedly (178).

(6) The sixth, through these [visions] arising as limitless, they become purified in their very essence.

(7) The seventh, through these [visions] arising as impure, it doesn't stop the origins of the ordinary world [*saṁsāra*].

(8) The eighth, through these [visions] arising as pure, primordial wisdom is connected to mother and son.

From knowing all these visions as self-appearing, you become liberated in the *dharmakāya*. In the *gSer gyi yang zhun* [*Refined Gold*] it says, "The visions of the three-fold embodiment of enlightenment are spontaneously present. Whatever arises is known as a dream or as an illusion. In that illusions are without inherent nature, you let go of attachment to them and let them be free. Set up [the mind] unobstructedly in emptiness/clarity. You most certainly will become liberated in the *dharmakāya*." According to this passage, at this time all the visions are gathered internally. The eight ways they dissolve happens instantaneously. As described elsewhere in the [*Refined Gold*] it says, "Compassion dissolves into compassion, just like when the sun sets and the light-rays [dissolve back into it]. You will have purified what is to be subdued and the agent subduing it. Light self-dissolves back into light, like a rainbow in the sky. Clarity and awakened awareness are non-dual.

The embodiment of enlightenment self-dissolves into the embodiment of enlightenment, much like the enlightened youthful vase body. Omniscience remains as internal clarity. Primordial wisdom dissolves into primordial wisdom, much like the son entering his mother's lap (179). Awakened awareness is liberated into its very own basis. Non-duality dissolves into non-duality, much like water dissolving into water. Subjective phenomena become mixed into one in the *dharmadhātu*. Limitless liberation dissolves into limitless liberation, much like space dissolving into space. Then you remain in a state of g.Yung drung [eternal] Bon. The impure [visions] dissolve into the pure [visions], like a tent collapsing by cutting the tent ropes. In a state of clear-light it is immovable. The pure [visions] dissolve in the gateway of primordial wisdom, like a lion that takes to the snowy mountains. You remain in this condition of g.Yung drung [eternal] Bon." According to this passage, the manner of dissolving these eight visions of [lively] awakened awareness like this reverses your [attachment] to sense-objects. Through staying in the inseparability of spontaneous presence and original purity, those who recognize this, thereafter will never turn back [to *saṁsāra*], and will take hold of their seat in *dharmakāya*. [All] *saṁsāra* and *nirvāṇa* dissolves in the expanse, and becomes liberated in the universal ground. You should recognize at this time the manner by which it dissolves spontaneously.

Any of these four [levels of visions] has special instructions in general.

2.4.3.2 Three Teachings 179

At the time that the three visions—ultimate sound, light, and light-rays—arise (180) as a welcoming party, remember the three teachings, which are like an escort:

(1) Whatever arises you must believe is self-appearing, without any doubt, at this time just as a mother and son meet.

(2) Other than this supreme belief, without any distraction, seize the throne, as in the metaphor of the unchangeable golden spoon.

(3) Establish immovably the basic disposition of having seized the throne and never come back to *saṁsāra*, using the metaphor of an arrow [shot] by a great archer that never comes back.

This completes the three essential points as one.

The [resultant] *Buddhahood* is described in the *Yang rtse* [*Epitome*] where it says, "[sNya chen Li shu sta ring said], 'For those *ḍākinī*s who are endowed with the right vessel through faith, and who have received the pointing out instructions at this time, it is no longer necessary to get stuck in the after-death *bardos*. When the three [favorable] conditions arise, these become the three welcoming parties, and the three escorts that guide you along. When completing all three essential points as one, liberation will come.'" So it is said.

2.4.3.3 Six Secondary Conditions that Remind You 180

The six secondary conditions to remember [in the after-death *bardo*] are:

(1) Seeing the visions of the *bardo* makes the [right] conditions for you to remember your *yi dam* [tutelary] deity, so you will see his or her face.

(2) From the admiration in which you remember your lama, he comes before you and shows you the pith instructions.

(3) Through remembering these instructions (181) you will know [everything] as self-arising/self-appearing.

(4) By that, through remembering the view,

(5) You will remember original purity of the expanse, and then

(6) You will remember it is necessary to stay concentrated on this, so liberation will come.

In the *gSer gyi zhun ma* [*Refined Gold*] it says, "Remembering your lama; remembering the instructions; remembering your *yi dam* [tutelary] deity; remembering [the view of]; remembering the primordial expanse; and then remembering to remain concentrated on emptiness."

At this time, in a way that they co-emerge, six paranormal abilities arise:

(1) Through having purified the sense-organs, the six sense systems become pure seeing.

(2) Through having purified sublime knowledge, you become free of analyzing with conceptual thought and the sense-mind.

(3) Through having purified primordial wisdom, you will know when all sentient beings of the three times will be born, stay, die, and transfer their consciousnesses.

(4) Through having purified *samādhi*, the mind has become serviceable.

(5) Through having exhausted the karmic outflows, having accomplished your own purpose, you can see the birth places of the six realms, and through that you are able to serve the purposes of others.

(6) Through having purified [all] knowledge, you are able to see according to the irreversible seeing of a *Buddha*. In the previous [text, *Refined Gold*] it says, "When the sense-faculty's seeing is purified, sublime knowledge occurs. By purifying primordial wisdom, and *samādhi*, and all conditioned outflows, you complete omniscience." According to this passage, those of best capacity bring liberation to full measure in three moments (182), those of middling capacity in five moments, and those of lesser capacity attain liberation in twenty-one moments.

Third, when they exhale their last breath in the innate emanating *Buddha*-fields, as before, when the visions arise as spontaneously present, because they are not liberated at that time, out of twenty-one moments, they are the last. When the *bardo* of rebirth arises like a dream, through seeing the [visions] in the gateways and being reminded of these as they wake up, those who did not previously recognize them in the *bardo* of *dharmadhātu*, will now wander[15] in the *bardo* of rebirth. By knowing that, at the present time, you can consider taking a rebirth in the innate emanating *Buddha*-fields. The way to be magically reborn is described in the *gSer gyi thur* [*Golden Spoon*] where it says, "Having recognized the *bardo* of rebirth, you will exhaust all habitual karmic propensities of being reborn in any of the six realms [of *saṁsāra*], and will exhale your last breath in innate emanating *Buddha*-fields. Through pure devotion and faith you make the connection in your next life and nothing remains [beyond that]. *E ma ho!*" So it is said.

2.4.3.4 Consciousness-Transference 182

At this point in time, awakened awareness is propelled like a shooting star, imagining it like a ball of light coming out from the Brahma aperture. At this point in time, [it is important] to remember these [innate emanating] *Buddha*-fields. Imagine awakened awareness in the form of a [seed-syllable] *A* (183) and put in the effort to propel [your mind] carefully again and again into the enlightened heart-mind of the principle [*Buddha*] of that realm.

The *Buddha*-field of the east is Manifest Joy, and the *Buddha* is gSal ba rang Byung. The *Buddha*-field of the north is Completely Supreme Actions, and the *Buddha* is dGe lha Gar phyug. The *Buddha*-field to the west is the Stacked Lotus *Buddha*- field and the *Buddha* is Bye brag dNgos med. The *Buddha*-field to the south is Splendorous State and the *Buddha* is Gga' ba Don 'grub. The *Buddha*-field in the center is Spontaneous Presence and the *Buddha* is 'Od dkar gNas 'dzin. These are the five wielders of the eternal swastika. Their respective retinues are born magically, including the male and female *bodhisattvas*, and each retinue has its respective color. Each of these respective principle [*Buddhas*] is teaching Bon to the surrounding retinue. All the places [in these *Buddha*] realms are made of precious jewels. There are emanated birds, deer, horses, elephants, and other animals. Each respective *Buddha*-field is matched to a specific color. There are trees [in the form of] multi-faceted jewels. There are rivers

---

15. Text has '*khyal pa*: "unconnected"; should be '*khyam pa*: "wander."

possessing the eight qualities. There is food and drink, and unimaginable possessions. In the directions above these *Buddha*-fields (184) are the emanating *Buddha*-fields of the wrathful deities called "igniting the fire of the wrathful deities of the *dharmadhātu*." Those born there will stay five hundred years [and after that they are] free of the *bardos* [and] will only attain Buddhahood.

[Different beings] have [a natural disposition toward] one of the five *Buddha*-fields of the five types of beings who travel along this lower path, like the *maṇḍala* of the wrathful deities, but these do not ultimately exist. These [various] *Buddha*-fields [exist] in your own heart, and become clear by themselves as the self-clarity of the five primordial wisdoms, such as emptiness primordial wisdom, and so forth. The *maṇḍala* of the wrathful deities resides primordially in the skull palace, and these appear, automatically manifesting. They are called "the innate emanating *Buddha*-fields."

Ordinary beings, who do not see these at the gateways through their having practiced Bon and mastering [all appearances] and illusions and dreams, are said to become liberated in the rebirth *bardo*. Those who are unfamiliar with Bon, through practicing devotional prayers, taking refuge, and having faith, will turn back [the possibility of] a bad rebirth, and can depend on meeting with and attaining a good rebirth (185). Having attained a good rebirth, they will meet with Bon [teachings] [and] they will attain emancipation.

All others than these are lost in the jaws of the rebirth *bardo*, and are impelled by the force of their previous karma. They continue to have happy, sad, and neutral feelings that come and stay and wander over and over again in an ocean of the limitless suffering in *saṁsāra*. Because they have been unsuitable [vessels], it is very important that they endeavor to take up virtue and abandon vice very carefully.

[Conclusion]

"All those who never move from the innate space of omniscient, primordial wisdom and the embodiment of enlightenment become the agents of expressing the vast truths of the *sūtras* and *tantras* and whatever is their stainless fruition. Their sacred foundation is the unending intelligence to explain this thoroughly with just a few words of elaboration. Having depended on this, sound the drum for these noble and renowned [teachings] of whomever is wise. From the lotus pond of my mind I generated the nectar of bliss for the benefit of sentient beings from one who was wise [enough to explain it to me]. It is not for everyone. For all those who have the divine eyes of omniscience, when they look, they see the very nature of reality. Thereafter, they will have established a little bit of the essence of this profound truth of the expanse/awakened awareness. Through that, if you know any of this well, (186) you become a great practitioner who goes after this great teaching. The way ordinary appearances arise in this world, and the entire army of afflictive emotions, becomes firewood that is burned to ashes in the fire [of these teachings]. [These teachings] are like a hundred thousand suns of primordial wisdom [that when it arises] dries up the ocean of suffering.

This is the secret supreme path. I imagined myself having the form of my lama, whose primordial wisdom [represents] both Kun tu bZang po and Kun tu bZang mo. It did not come from the realization of what had not yet been realized, but by awakening from [the influence of] previous karmic actions. It happened like this. Even though [these teachings] on the essence of the natural state are very profound and subtle, it is a [subject] that is very difficult [to understand]. I did not rely on a wise teacher, and in my childhood I didn't study, but still I wrote it down. Here, it is possible to be deluded and mistaken. For that reason, it is not for an ordinary being who has an immature mind. Whatever bad deeds I did I am confessing in front of the *Buddha* and his sons [*bodhisattvas*] who have the sharpest intelligence. Whatever wholesome accumulated merit has come from this emanates thousands of lights. [May] these profound and vast gShen teachings arise forever in the expanse, with the blazing splendor of the visions of the light of primordial wisdom. The essence of its original purity, great emptiness, thoroughly destroys the thick darkness of the existing world [that comes from] not recognizing [awakened awareness] (187). May everyone take an everlasting, enlightened, youthful vase body, whose inherent nature is spontaneously present. Those who have cause to remain attached to family and friends are trapped in the cage [of *saṁsāra*]. It is quite certain that they will be free from the marvels of the everyday world, seen as a dream that is without essence. Those who are tightly caught in their mind-streams by the lasso of fame and greatness in this world, when they transfer consciousness [at the time of death], the visions on the other side become uncertain, arising from the influence of pleasant, unpleasant, and neutral karma. Those who know all of this as the nature of what is caused by oneself, as the immense fire in which we are consumed, [and also] know the place in the peaceful jungle where one stays like the [precious and rare] *udumvara* flower [an isolated meditation place], and who take hold of the biographies of the holy lamas, are eligible for these teachings as a life-long companion. I said these words to my followers who had a fortunate karmic connection, "Take these [precious] instructions into your hearts."

Here is a place that is devoid of any worldly activities whatsoever, on the side of a mountain, which has dancing trees. No one made it. It is well set up. This good house of rock is near the unceasing sound of the waterfall. When I hear the melodies of this lovely flock of birds, [they seem] to be praising me (188). Walking around in this place, it looks like heaven shifted here, and after coming here, it seems like the gods are scattering flowers. Friendships are useless. It is a great place where everything grows. All the fortune of this world is here, and you can do whatever you want. In this valley of herbal medicines, a lot of very peaceful ducks reside. There is none of the unpleasantness of the world. This is the place where I find great peace. Far away from the busyness of the everyday world, I was able to set in stone the heart-essence of the Great Completion meditation.

These [teachings] are for people who dwell here all the time in accordance with their meditation experience, who make their pillows wet [by crying after being moved by the meditation experiences]. I am the *yogi* who is prepared to serve the purpose of sentient beings, so that this might happen a little. I have shown here all the instructions that are very famous in all the three realms. Those who meet with these are of fortunate karma. May they stay in the state of primordial clear-light!"

These teachings were written at the urging of holy g.Yung drung mThong grol rtsal, who is an emanation of rJe brtsun Byang ba Khro tshang, who also is an accomplished retreat master, and especially by the Bya btang sprul sku Tshe dbang 'gyur med (189) who urged me [to compose this] by offering this paper. Rig pa rang shar, who is the *yogi* of the highest vehicle, at the place where the three roots of the *ḍākinī*s are assembled, called g.Yung drung lhun po ri'i dga' tshal, in the summer my dwelling there was a tent of rainbow light, arising in circular, upward-lifted spokes, and semicircular shapes. In the winter a rain of flowers directly falls. The trees extract sunlight from their tops, and drink moisture from their roots. The trunk is conch [white]. The bark is copper-colored. The branches and leaves extend [everywhere]. Golden fruit ripens. When it ripens, its nectar emits a fragrance. When it rains, they all smell of the fragrance of camphor. Many [fruits] are amassed. Inside my secret place [hermitage], when the sun shines, the pale blue looks like maidens smiling with their eyes, which gives happiness to my heart. On top of the trees you can hear the melodies of many types of lovely birds (190) continuously coming forth.

Groups of genuine *yogis* are arranged around this place. Here at [a place called] Gu ge I wrote this from my own heart. Through composing these words of supreme sublime knowledge, I am illuminating Great Completion teachings. May they continually spread!

OM SVA STI

Immovable from the original purity of the primordial universal basis, [may you attain] omniscience, supreme primordial wisdom, and embodiment of enlightenment of a primordial *Buddha*. May you attain the queen of the youthful vase-body self-appearing from its depths of clarity. Homage to the forefathers, those Victorious Ones of the three times. This is the secret Bon of the oral transmission lineage and its enlightened intention. This is the vast path that extracts the milk from the ocean of the three series of Great Completion [teachings]. This is a wide and good path of few words. May Rig par Rang shar, who is the master of teaching everything, be victorious! This is the foundation of the vast ocean of eternal Bon. This is the highest fruition vehicle, which is like refined gold.

For those with fortunate karma and of best capacity, these [teachings] are the precious jewels of the heart. They are not shown to everyone. The powerful ones are not afraid of anything (191). Therefore, in the sky of vast intelligence, adorned with the clouds of hearing and reflecting on the teachings, whose splendorous form does much for the benefit of others, may they bring about the thunder of realization and *samādhi* for those who travel [this path]. This is the lama who makes the rain of the best teachings. Even the chief who strives along the stages of the eight vehicles can't see this ultimate truth, which is beyond the three times and the mind. Dri med sNying po, through the vital essence of his enlightened intention, shows this as bare, naked, enlightened intention that is effortless self-liberation. Therefore, this is the gateway of thousands of great minds.

This was printed by Tshul khrims g.yung drung. He gave the materials out of the inexhaustible generosity of the teachings. Make a welcome party to the future [generations] of fortunate ones, namely those who have accumulated pure virtue for these [teachings] on behalf of the realm of sentient beings who have amassed the darkness of the three realms. May they conquer the accumulated darkness of not recognizing awakened awareness in the expanse of peace. May all of you give up your last breaths going to sacred emancipation. This colophon was written by Shes rab mChog ldan, a close disciple of [Sha rdza Rinpoche]. The letters were carved in wood by Tshul khrims bStan 'dzin dbang po.

Bibliography

Lopon Tenzin Namdak (1993). *Heart Drops of Dharmakaya, Dzogchen Practice of the Bon Tradition*. Translation and commentary. Ithaca, NY: Snow Lion.

Shar rdza bKra shis rGyal mtshan (1990). *Shar rdza bKa' 'bum*. [Collected works of Shar rdza] *'od gsal rdzogs pa chen po'i lam gyi rim pa'i khrid yig kun tu bzang po snying rtig ces bya bzhugs* [Heart Drops of Kun tu bZang Po; A Practical Guide on the Stages of the Path of Great Completion] Chamdo, 16 volumes. Volume 10, pages 77-191. Block print version.

www.ingramcontent.com/pod-product-compliance
Lightning Source LLC
Chambersburg PA
CBHW062057280426
43673CB00085B/458/J